D1583158

HIGHLAND WILDERNESS

COLIN PRIOR

'Nor does the scenery any more affect the thoughts than the thoughts affect the scenery. We see places through our humour as through different coloured glasses. We are ourselves a term in the equation, a note of the chord, and make discord or harmony almost at will.'

ROBERT LOUIS STEVENSON

HIGHLAND WILDERNESS

COLIN PRIOR

INTRODUCTIONS BY MAGNUS LINKLATER

CONSTABLE • LONDON

FOR GERALDINE, ALEXANDRA AND LAURENCE

CONSTABLE & ROBINSON
3 THE LANCHESTERS
162 FULHAM PALACE ROAD
LONDON W6 9ER
WWW.CONSTABLEROBINSON.COM

THIS EDITION PUBLISHED IN THE UK IN 2004 BY CONSTABLE,
AN IMPRINT OF CONSTABLE & ROBINSON LTD

FIRST PUBLISHED IN THE UK IN 1993 BY CONSTABLE & COMPANY LTD

COPYRIGHT © 2004 IN PHOTOGRAPHS AND CAPTIONS: COLIN PRIOR
COPYRIGHT © 2004 IN INTRODUCTIONS: MAGNUS LINKLATER
COPYRIGHT © 2004 CONSTABLE & ROBINSON LTD

ALL RIGHTS RESERVED. THIS BOOK IS SOLD SUBJECT TO THE
CONDITION THAT IT SHALL NOT, BY WAY OF TRADE OR OTHERWISE, BE
LENT, RE-SOLD, HIRED OUT OR OTHERWISE CIRCULATED IN ANY FORM
OF BINDING OR COVER OTHER THAN THAT IN WHICH IT IS PUBLISHED
AND WITHOUT A SIMILAR CONDITION INCLUDING THIS CONDITION
BEING IMPOSED ON THE SUBSEQUENT PURCHASER.

A COPY OF THE BRITISH LIBRARY CATALOGUING IN PUBLICATION DATA
IS AVAILABLE FROM THE BRITISH LIBRARY.

ISBN 1-84529-065-8

10 9 8 7 6 5 4 3 2 1

PRINTED IN ITALY

CONTENTS

INTRODUCTION

Images of the Highlands can vary as widely as the hills themselves. The photographs in the following pages – so lovingly and skilfully created by Colin Prior – reveal a beauty that is at times ethereal. There are scenes of golden peaks, caught in the dying sun; a stretch of water scintillating under a shaft of light; dawn rising over hazy blue islands. Many capture the image of an untouched and uninhabited place, nature rampant, apparently changeless, little sign of man's intrusion. And for many people that is indeed the Highlands, an ideal to be cherished. Conserving what one writer has called that 'heroic sense of beauty and subtlety in nature' has become a vital cause in an age where everywhere the environment is threatened.

And yet, the Highlands are more complex than that, and if the true character of their wild places is to be understood, their past history and future prospects need to be explored and explained. This is not, in fact, a savage or untamed land. It is a lived-in place, one that has been vastly changed by those who have inhabited it. It has seen the trees which once covered it disappear, the people who built houses in its remote glens retreat, the sheep and deer transform its vegetation, industry alter its coast and seascape. Sometimes, looking back at the changing face of the Highlands, it seems as if only the rocks truly remain.

It is the origin of those rocks that give the Scottish Highlands their shape and their sense of drama. Geologists have often commented that Scotland has more varieties of stone within its boundaries than many other larger countries. Some, known as 'terranes' – great slices of the earth's crust, each with its own different character – collided and fused to form one plate along the fault-lines that bisect the land. The blocks which are the Grampian Mountains and the Northern Highland were created more than 400 million years ago, sliding into place along the Great Glen fault. But they are mere striplings compared to the older rocks of Islay and Jura, whose layers of antiquity reveal that, more than 700 million years ago, Scotland had no fewer than 17 different ice ages. Then, further north, in Lewis, there is the hardest and oldest rock of all – Lewisian Gneiss, some 3000 million years old, forced up to the surface from many miles beneath, by unimaginable pressures. This is part of the earth's original core, the foundation of all rocks.

Some sense of that unfathomable ancientness can be gathered from Colin's pictures of the north-western Highlands. He shows the Torridon Hills in Wester Ross, rising from the cobalt blue of the loch that divides them, and here, you might imagine, are more of these primitive hills. But this pink sandstone came later – if you climb amongst its jagged peaks, you will find yourself treading on deposits left on top of the original rock by rivers that flowed through the landscape 1500 million years later.

Then, more recently – barely 25,000 years ago – great glaciers carved their way through this porous rock, boring down through many thousands of feet, to reveal the Lewisian Gneiss beneath.

Volcanoes, glaciers, earthquakes and tidal waves have formed the face of the Highlands and given it the foundations of its beauty. Once clothed in forest, these hills and moors are now more likely to be coloured by moorland grass, by heather or by bracken – and, of course, by water which reflects back the constantly changing scene around it. What Colin's pictures show is the way that light illuminates the landscape in all its infinite variety. Scotland's weather is something of a national joke – rain, with occasional interruptions of rain, is the standard image. That is wholly misleading. It is the unexpected and the changeable nature of the weather that is the Highlands' greatest asset. There are more majestic landscapes elsewhere – the Swiss Alps towering over the lake of Geneva, for instance, or the desert areas of Arizona – but they are seen in a static light, one which changes perhaps only twice a day, at dawn and dusk. In the Highlands, nothing stays the same. A passing rain-storm will lift to reveal a sudden snatch of sun bathing the bracken beneath in dazzling gold. A mist, wrapped around the summit of a hill, will drift away, leaving a wisp of white hanging over the deep purple of the heather underneath. A brilliant blue sky illuminates a snow-covered peak, and then is closed off by the blackest of clouds, transforming a summer idyll into a scene of dark foreboding. The richness of the tapestry is constantly renewed.

The hills themselves, as Colin has followed them, change steadily across the country. His odyssey begins in the rounded gentleness of the southern Highlands and culminates in the sharp cliff-edges of the Hebrides. There is an early photograph of Beinn Dorain, near Bridge of Orchy, which shows the dawn spreading a pink light over the snow-covered shoulder of this majestic mountain. With these gentle curves and sloping contours, you might almost imagine yourself in the Scottish Borders, where the landscape is all hill pasture and spruce plantations. And yet this is unmistakably Highland country. Turn now to the fortress hills that protect the entrance to Glencoe, the Buachaille Etive Mor in the central Highlands, lit by a late evening sun, its harsh edges riven by ancient scars, rearing up off the barren plain that is the Rannoch Moor. This is the Highlands of ancient memory, a place where the clans survived against the odds, threatened by violence from their enemies and by an unforgiving climate. The mountains seem to reflect something of their defiance and their ultimate defeat. A place that once supported a thousand people, is now empty of human dwellings. The rocks live on.

The sea defines the Highlands as much as the hills themselves, whether it is the penetration of the long sea lochs – which elsewhere would be called fjords – along its western coast, the towering cliffs of Sutherland and the Hebrides, or the miles of gold and silver sand which mark its edges. The coastline of Scotland is some 6000 miles (10,000 kilometres) long, and Colin's photographs trace it from the gale-lashed outcrops of Easdale, the slate island on Scotland's west coast, to the gentle beaches of Newburgh on the eastern shore; past waves crashing onto the cliffs at St Cyrus, then on to the emerald green of Gruinard Bay on the west, the mirror-calm of Loch Duich, reflecting magically the Five Sisters of Kintail, the vanishing horizons of the Atlantic, seen from the Island of Eigg, and the endless sands of Luskentyre on Harris, where you can walk for miles without seeing a soul.

It is this emptiness that defines the term wilderness, and yet it is not a wilderness in the proper sense, since many thousands of people work and live there. The great post-war debate in Scotland has revolved around how best to preserve its beauty and its wildness, while still allowing access to the many thousands of visitors who wish to explore it, and support the human population for which it is home. Because it is a magnet to walkers, climbers, bikers and canoeists, who flock in ever-increasing numbers to breathe the air of 'the last great unexploited lung of Europe', there have been growing concerns about their impact on the landscape. Although it is ancient and rugged, as we have seen, it is fragile nevertheless. Tracks and footpaths become easily eroded, litter is left, rare species of plants, birds and animals are threatened by large numbers of ramblers.

The challenge has grown steadily more daunting as the number of people demanding access to the once remote areas of the north has increased. 'Visitor pressure' is the current jargon, and though recreation and the encouragement of ever more sightseers are seen as the key to local employment and the future of the economy, the growth in numbers poses, in some areas at least, a real threat to the very environment the visitors have come to enjoy.

Most people who come to the Highlands have in their minds an idea of wildness, and for some it is fixed by the memories of a particular day. I have two pictures that stand out. One is of Kintail, on a day of searing heat in June, high on the green hills that form the Five Sisters, where we came across a spring, bubbling unexpectedly below the tops; the water was clear and icy cold, and I can still remember the first sharp taste of it. The second memory is of lying amongst blueberries on Stac Polly, looking down on to Loch Lurgainn, where the surface was of an almost unimaginable turquoise.

In neither of these memories can I recall the intrusion of other people. Empty hills, deserted beaches, open waters, these were the norm. Yet now, Stac Pollaidh displays a deep and angry scar, chiselled cruelly into its southern slope, where climbers mount in single file; and you cannot reach the tops of the Five Sisters on a summer's afternoon without jostling your way past fellow-walkers. The nearer the centres of population, the greater, of course, the threat. Around Loch Lomond, pleasure-ground for generations of Glaswegians, there are muddy tracks on the hills, trodden by thousands of walkers; caravans, litter and the sheer weight of people impose almost intolerable burdens on the natural surroundings; while on the loch itself the roar of speedboats in summer becomes the dominant sound. Without protective measures, such places might simply have become, in time, rural slums.

To confront this challenge the Nature Conservancy Council, for long regarded in Scotland as an autocratic body, run from Peterborough in England, was merged in 1992 with the Countryside Commission and replaced by the Scottish Natural Heritage Agency, headed by the broadcaster and naturalist, Magnus Magnusson, and sited in Scotland. It regarded itself originally as a facilitating body, bringing together the many vested interests in the Highlands, and trying to get them to work together in the interests of conservation – 'getting hold of the people who manage the ground', as Magnusson put it. He believed that intervention was the last resort, and argued that co-operation was far more effective. He recoiled from the word 'wilderness' because it implied an area emptied of people. 'If you don't have people on the ground, you can't manage it,' he says.

Increasingly, however, it became clear that stronger legislation would be needed if the conservation of the Highlands was to work properly. Some places are hardy, rugged and perfectly capable of resisting the impact of hill-walkers and climbers. Torridon would probably fall into this category. So too would Glencoe, managed by the National Trust for Scotland and watched over by its mentor, the mountaineer Hamish MacInnes, who is a great encourager of visitors. Others are more vulnerable, and it was with them in mind that the arguments for national parks came back into focus during the tenure of the present Chairman of Scottish Natural Heritage, John Markland. The idea of creating National Parks as a way of protecting the Highlands goes back at

least 100 years. Whereas in England and Wales they have been introduced without great opposition, in Scotland there has been enormous resistance. The very idea of attempting to tame this wild and natural landscape by restricting access, making paths, employing rangers and wardens, posting notices and drawing up rules and regulations, was held to be hostile to the very essence of the Highlands. At least as persuasive was the claim that National Parks, far from controlling numbers, would actively increase them. They would, said critics of the idea, become 'honey-pots', attracting yet more visitors and further threatening a fragile environment.

As tourism grew in the 1970s and 1980s, the pressure for change became irresistible. With the introduction of devolution, Scotland acquired the means to introduce it. The new Scottish Parliament, established in 1999 following a referendum which gave it enthusiastic backing, introduced a National Parks Act a year later. It placed the interests of people at the centre of its aims, which were fourfold: to conserve and enhance the natural heritage of the Highlands, to promote sustainable use of their resources, to promote understanding and enjoyment of their special qualities, and to encourage sustainable economic and social development. The first place to qualify was Loch Lomond and Trossachs, perhaps the most popular and celebrated area of all the Highlands, which attracts five million visitors a year.

In 2002, the Loch Lomond and Trossachs National Park was introduced. Funded by the Scottish Executive, and run by a 25-strong council, it has begun the work of protecting the area, while balancing the needs of local farmers and residents. Sustainable development remains the watchword, and all lovers of the Highlands will be watching anxiously to see whether this can be delivered.

Fifty miles to the north, in the Cairngorms, the Highlands' second National Park came into being in September 2003. Covering 1400 square miles (3600 square kilometres), it is the largest in Britain. The case here was, if anything, more urgent. Designated as a possible World Heritage Site, the Cairngorm Mountains contain a quarter of Scotland's native woodlands and its largest area of natural vegetation, as well as 25 per cent of Britain's threatened species. Rare mosses and lichens, birds like the ptarmigan and the dotterel, and animals like the white hare were all threatened by growing numbers of walkers and climbers. The area had long been regarded by the naturalists Desmond Nethersole-Thompson and Adam Watson as desperately in need of protection from those who regularly invaded it. Some 20 years ago, they wrote:

The challenge we face in the Cairngorms is how best to decide between immediate and long-term priorities. Nothing is yet irretrievably lost … But the wonderful tops and plateaux are already at greater risk than at any time since the last ice age. And down in the valleys many of the grandest relics of the Old Caledonian Forest are steadily disappearing and heading for extinction. Time is short, and fast running out.'

So finally, the argument for a Cairngorm National Park was won. An agonized debate had already taken place over the chair-lift which took thousands of visitors up Cairngorm itself. By allowing them instant access to its heights, it was encouraging the very erosion that threatened the area. Finally, a decision was taken to build a funicular railway, which would allow them to view the grandeur of the scenery, but would ensure that they were properly controlled. Again, it seemed an intrusion into the very naturalness which lends the Highlands their essential charm, but practicalities and the need for protection took precedence.

The organization that has been central to these developments has been Scottish Natural Heritage. Its decisions have not been without controversy. Most land in Scotland is privately owned, and most landowners believe that they are at least as well-informed about the best way of looking after their acres of moorland or loch as any outside body. They argue, too, that it is they who provide employment, and that simply designating sites of special interest, or environmentally sensitive areas, does little to provide jobs. Since SNH responds not only to government policy, but to directives drawn up by the European authorities in Brussels, there has been a consequent growth in bureaucracy which irritates private owners almost as much as those who have to administer it.

One typical example has been the control of deer. SNH is pledged, amongst other things, to the regeneration of natural species, such as the original Caledonian pine, and in most places this can only be achieved by a drastic reduction in the number of deer. The Deer

Commission, which is responsible for ensuring that damage caused by deer is reduced, attempts to ensure that numbers are kept in balance with all the other, often conflicting interests of land use – such as farming, forestry, tourism, field sports and hill-walking. However, it is a struggle to keep abreast of rising numbers. There are no accurate figures for the number of deer in Scotland. One statistic suggests that there are 300,000 red deer – those superb creatures which can be seen occasionally on the skyline of a hill, or wheeling in great herds across a corrie. But that only accounts for those that can be counted on open ground. Many more are hidden within forests, and when you add in the roe deer, the sika and the fallow, that figure may need to be doubled.

For all their beauty, they are increasingly seen as modern predators. In some areas, such as the Cairngorms, the size of the deer population (as many as 150 deer per square kilometre) has become incompatible with attempts to regenerate the forest. Short of fencing them out of specified areas, or literally decimating some of the herds (one estimate suggests that a population of 10,000 deer on the Mar Lodge/Invercauld area would have to be reduced to 1000), it is hard to see how trees can re-grow naturally. The advance of the deer is partly to do with the value of sporting rights on an estate. Deer are, after all, a significant contributor to the Highland economy in the form of venison and the high prices which visitors are prepared to pay to shoot them. This sporting income is one of the few direct tourist contributions to the cost of land management, and has helped pay for stalkers,

gamekeepers and other employees in the remoter rural areas where employment is not always easy to find. Landowners are, not surprisingly, against the mass culling of their deer, but it is they who are at least partly responsible for the growth in numbers. As the cost of running estates has risen, so local employment has been cut back. It was the skill and experience of people who had grown up on the land which traditionally kept the size of the deer herds in check. The loss of their accumulated local knowledge on such matters as culling hinds, burning heather, or controlling vermin, is a serious one. Meanwhile, a succession of mild winters has exacerbated the problem.

Issues such as these continue to divide the Highlands. Colin's camera hovers over the battleground, and the beauty he reveals gives added urgency to questions about its future. What should be conserved of this priceless area? The Highlands as they are now? The Highlands as they might once have been? Or the Highlands as they should be? And who is to determine precisely what that ideal state really is? Part of the strong emotional appeal this vast and rugged landscape exerts on many of us stems from an almost palpable sense of loss, a nostalgia for the days when the land was less spoiled, when people inhabited the glens, when there was what we think of as a balance between man and nature. There never was such a golden age, of course, and striving to recreate it is probably a lost cause. But to reach some kind of accommodation between the demands of the human race and those of the natural environment remains the goal of all who love the fragile landscape of the Highlands. And it is only by studying its past history that we can properly reach some understanding of how it has evolved, and how best it might be preserved.

For generations the Highlands have aroused passionate argument. Blood has been shed in their name, great suffering has been caused as their people have moved, whether forced by fellow humans, a relentless economy, or both, from the hills to the coast, and thence into exile. The past can sometimes be discerned in the form of ancient cultivation, still visible in the strips of green that run down deep straths, or the sad piles of stone which once housed human beings. Much that has been written of the Highland landscape casts it in the role of an idyll under threat, a paradise with the enemy at the gate. Its poetry is shot through with sadness, whether it is the grandness of the epic that mourns the passing of the Lords of the Isles – 'It is no joy without Clan Donald, it is no strength to be without them' – or the elegiac verses of Duncan Ban Macintyre who was alive when the sheep first came to Argyll and Perthshire and who saw the threat they posed to the Highland way of life.

Early accounts by travellers in the Highlands are less sentimental. Some, like Martin Martin, a native of Skye, who wrote of the western islands in the late seventeenth century, saw a land which was reasonably productive and a small but healthy population. But even then, he wrote, the people were desperately vulnerable to the famines which were a regular and unpredictable part of agricultural life. Others, who came from further afield, were often appalled at what they took to be the grinding poverty of highland life. Duncan Forbes of Culloden, writing in the early part of the next century, was shocked by the crass forms of agriculture that he saw. On Tiree he wrote of the 'ridiculous processes of husbandry which almost utterly destroys the island' – corn being pulled up by the roots, weeds everywhere, straw burnt rather than used as fodder. A correspondent of *The Scotsman*, visiting the village of Torren more than a hundred years later, in 1877, wrote:

At the top of the village, gathered in a listless way on a bit of moss land before an almost ruinous cottage, were a dozen children – as squalid and as miserable as any that could be produced from the innermost dens of the Cowgate … This sorrowful index to the condition of the crofter forces itself very strongly on a stranger's notice as he passes through this island.

And even the beauty of the landscape failed to impress. Edward Burt, an English officer who wrote of his journeys in the north of Scotland in the 1720s, presented a decidedly unromantic view of the dark landscape through which he travelled: 'The eye penetrates far among them, and sees more particularly their stupendous bulk, frightful irregularity, and horrid gloom, made yet more sombrous by the shades and faint reflections they communicate one to another.' Dr Johnson, coming to the Highlands fifty years later, wrote off the scenery as a 'wide extent of hopeless sterility'.

It was only later, in the nineteenth century, that the mountains and the lochs began to be appreciated. Victorian trippers wrote about them, drew them, rhapsodized over their waterfalls and their deep ravines, or, as Queen Victoria put it, 'the absence of hotels and beggars'. Walter Scott's narrative poem, The Lady of the Lake, was a kind of nineteenth-century guidebook to the beauties of the Highland landscape. J.M.W. Turner gave the hills, glens and ruined castles a romantic touch which has survived ever since, while Landseer took them to the point of parody.

Few of those who wrote made much mention of the great changes that were affecting the landscape even then. Commercial tree-felling had already altered much of the appearance of the western Highlands and the Grampians, and Thomas Pennant, who journeyed north as early as 1769, marvelled at the prices to be made from cutting down the great Caledonian pines: Mr Farquharson of Invercauld, he wrote, had just felled 800 of them, upwards of 200 years old, and had sold them for 'five-and-twenty shillings each'. Two types of forest had once swathed the hills, though the tree-line usually stopped wherever wind and height dictated: at about 2000 feet (600 metres) in the eastern Grampians, dropping to below 1000 feet (300 metres) in the western Highlands. Everywhere there had been pinewood with birch or the broad-leafed deciduous forest of oak with birch and alder, growing densely across the Highland land mass, only thinning on the coast where salt and wind discouraged it. Deforestation, however, began almost as soon as the first prehistoric man fashioned the first flint axe and strapped it to a shaft before hacking at the nearest tree trunk. As agriculture developed properly, serious inroads were made into the thick Highland woodland. The pace quickened in the Middle Ages when forests were burnt to clear them of wolves and because they provided harbour for outlaws. Timber was cut to prepare fields for planting and to build houses and ships.

As early as the fifteenth century, the loss of woodland was being seen as a risk, and legislation was introduced in the Scots Parliament to limit tree-felling. But it had little effect, and the demands of industry, whether in foundries, which needed charcoal, or from ships and roofs which needed timber, steadily cleared what remained of the dense forest areas. In Strathspey during the eighteenth century, the York Buildings Company specialized in buying up forfeited estates, building sawmills and foundries, cutting acres of trees, and dragging them to the river where they were floated down to Kingston on the river estuary. Forty-seven ships were built there during the Napoleonic wars alone.

The great Caledonian Forest, so lamented today, had in fact largely disappeared by the eighteenth century, though remnants of it survived in the Cairngorms, Strathspey and the Great Glen. There are glimpses of them in Colin's pictures. Any chance it had of natural regeneration was ended by the introduction of sheep.

Towards the middle of the eighteenth century, it was found that sheep could winter out of doors, even in the north, and with the introduction of turnips as winter fodder at the same time, the size of the herds grew, black-faced sheep being favoured over the small white-faced native breed. Steadily they replaced cattle, which were more labour-intensive, and began to alter significantly the vegetation of the uplands. It was not only that sheep cropped the tree seedlings and prevented the natural regeneration of the forest, but that whole areas of woodland were burnt down to provide sheep runs on a massive scale. 'Fire and tooth between them are invincible in preventing regeneration of forest,' commented the twentieth-century naturalist, Frank Fraser Darling.

For a time the burning back produced pasture for the herds which spread rapidly through the glens. But it led, just as in Brazil today, to longer-term infertility. As the chemical and organic cycle, which had always taken place beneath the cover of forest, was interrupted and brought to an end, so erosion also took place. Hill-cover was washed down from the tops, leaving the upper slopes bare and exposed; as the topsoil was carried downwards on to the flats beneath, the long natural processes which formed the peatlands were accelerated; bracken, which had been kept in check largely by the cattle whose hoofs broke and bruised it, began to spread; and the coarse grasses which had once provided grazing, but which were too tough for the sheep, now grew everywhere; heather rather than trees became the dominant vegetation.

It is ironic that much of what constitutes the beauty of the Highlands today – black-faced sheep grazing contentedly amidst the purple of the heather, the gold of the autumn bracken, scree on a Sutherland hill-slope, or the eerie space of a Caithness moor – stems from changes to the natural state of things brought about largely by man. Today they would be accounted an environmental disaster. Accommodating people while at the same time attempting to preserve the environment has taxed some of the best minds brought to bear on the problem over the past century. One extreme view was voiced by a policy adviser to the Prime Minister in 1979, as recorded by Professor Alastair Hetherington of Stirling University:

Does it matter if Ardnamurchan, Applecross and West Sutherland become uninhabited? If people choose to live in such places, why shouldn't they pay something closer to the economic cost of the services they require? Why should taxpayers in Manchester, Derby, Nottingham and Southampton have to subsidize them? Will anything be lost if those areas revert to wilderness?

That position, perhaps not intended entirely seriously, would fall down on several obvious counts. Firstly, no civilized modern state can simply abandon one part of its territory and allow its standard of living to drift hopelessly behind another's, without causing a basic social instability. And secondly, if that territory happens to be itself a priceless asset, it requires nurturing rather than neglect.

It was John Muir, one of the first and greatest of conservationists, a Scot from Dunbar in East Lothian, who first proposed a way forward for such territories. He had seen the destruction of the redwood and pine forests of the High Sierra in California, and realized that if their remnants were to be preserved, then special areas, protected by man for man, would have to be created. The National Park at Yosemite is his most famous legacy, but he left too a notion of how the wilderness he loved so much should be regarded. As John Morton Boyd, first Director of the Nature Conservancy Council, put it: '… not a place of savagery to be tamed, nor of waste to be transformed for profit, nor a curse to be shunned and feared, but a sacred place of natural renewal and adjustment and a civilizing influence upon all mankind.'

Living up to that ideal was a test for many of the twentieth-century ecologists who followed Muir. His principal disciple in Scotland was Fraser Darling, whose *West Highland Survey* is still a classic of keen observation and shrewd analysis. He was already convinced that national parks should be introduced to Scotland. There was a time in the 1950s when five designated areas, examined by a National Parks Committee, could have been acquired for around £3.5 million or just 50p an acre. Nevertheless, though national parks were established in England and Wales, there was no equivalent enthusiasm in Scotland. The failure to establish them at the time was, in Fraser Darling's view, a lost opportunity. 'Scotland has been left as the only nation of any consequence, civilized or not, that is without a system of national parks,' he wrote, '… planning, land apportionment and landscaping are being neglected to the detriment of the working capital of the Highlands, which is its scenery.'

At the time, his ideas were officially ignored by the Scottish Office which had commissioned him to write it. He was perhaps too idealistic in suggesting that the Highlands could be significantly repopulated, to establish a working environment for people living in harmony with the wildlife he loved. And he was perhaps too uncompromising in his conclusion that '… the bald unpalatable fact is emphasized that the Highlands and Islands are largely a devastated terrain, and that any policy which ignores this fact cannot hope to achieve rehabilitation.'

This will strike many people today, not least the Highlanders themselves, as an extreme description of the land they live in. Not least because the wilderness that Colin's photographs reveal is ever-changing. Now it is the sheep which are in retreat as the economy of hill-farming deteriorates. A new agricultural deal, worked out in Brussels, is aimed at helping farmers manage the landscape rather than simply breeding more animals, but no one is yet sure how this will affect the more remote of Scotland's rural areas. Perhaps the greatest post-war change to the appearance of the Highlands, has been the commercial planting of forests. Instead of birch and alder, these new plantations march in serried rows of Sitka spruce, fast-growing, but uniform in outline, alien to the natural landscape and to much of its wildlife. The Forestry Commission is dedicated to ensuring that the disastrous policies which allowed this to happen are replaced over the next few decades with a better balance of tree planting, ensuring that there are more mixed woodlands, with mature trees in tune with their surroundings. However, it has a long way to go to redress the depredations of the past, and meanwhile too much of Highland scenery is marred by the regimented squares which march over its hill-ground.

But if man-made creations have often been the villains of the piece, so man himself has also been the victim. The people's battle for their territory, to keep it, live on it, protect and cultivate it, has been, for much of Highland history, a losing one. The land has always been poor, economically fragile and agriculturally marginal. The history of its crofting community can be read as a continuous and often despairing attempt to hold on to land against the odds, and to cudgel a living from it in the face of disaster after disaster – whether natural or man-made.

Land, its ownership, theft, retrieval, cultivation, conservation and despoliation, is the running theme throughout the history of the Highlands, and it remains at the heart of the debate about their future today. In James Hunter's classic work, *The Making of the Crofting Community*, the villain of the piece is usually the landlord, rapacious, cruel and greedy, seizing every opportunity to raise profits at the expense of his people and their lives. But closer scrutiny of events suggests that it was frequently the landlord, whether clan chief or laird, who was himself the victim – forced to the brink of bankruptcy and beyond in an effort to maintain his people on land that simply did not have the resources to sustain them. Lord Macdonald spent all his capital during the potato famine of 1846 maintaining his clansmen on

North Uist; Robertsons, Mackenzies of Cromarty and Lovats refused to move their people, despite conditions of great hardship, some even taking in refugees from neighbouring estates; and Macleods of Dunvegan drove themselves to penury in the mid-nineteenth century in order to keep 8000 of their tenants on the land, preferring to face ruin than let them starve. Even the second Duke of Sutherland, whose agents, James Loch and Patrick Sellar, were responsible for some of the most brutal of the clearances under the much-vilified first Duke early in the nineteenth century, spent £8000 (say £250,000 at today's value) on famine relief.

It was during this century that the general shift of the Highland population from the hills and glens to the coastal regions took place. There, fishing and kelping – gathering seaweed which, when incinerated, provided potash and soda for the manufacture of glass, soap and dye – helped for a time to supplement the meagre living that was to be got from the much poorer land at sea-level. For about fifty years kelping afforded employment for thousands of people (3000 in Orkney alone), albeit for desperately low wages. But as so often with the Highland economy, developments elsewhere undermined the industry. Cheaper substitutes were found, and the abolition of duties on imported material made the transport south of kelp unviable. Fishing, in particular the herring industry, lasted longer, with the great expansion of the herring fleets in the mid-nineteenth century offering employment to crofters, both men and womenfolk, not only for catching but for curing the fish. For a time it seemed as if fishing would be the saving of the Highlands since there were summer jobs to be had as well as winter employment on the boats; but this industry too fell victim, partly to its own success as record catches drove prices down, but also to the imposition of import duties, this time by European countries anxious to protect their own markets. In 1887, it was estimated that about £40,000 was lost to the crofting population of Lewis alone because of the slump in the herring industry, and the average wage brought back from the east-coast fishings, where the Lewismen went for work in the summer, fell from £20 or £30 in the early 1880s to just £1 or £2.

The introduction of the potato as the staple diet of the Highlander in the 1740s meant that there was an ability to weather the occasional failures of the grain harvest and support the population at a reasonably steady level until the first appearance of the potato disease a century later. Massive famine relief operations sent north from Glasgow, Edinburgh and London meant that relatively few died, but again the vulnerability of the local economy was exposed.

Despite all these setbacks, the population of the Highlands climbed in the first half of the nineteenth century, and was actually higher at the end of it than it had been at the beginning. The worst periods of population drift did not take place during the clearances, the decline of the kelping industry, the slump in the herring trade, or the potato famine, but later, during the depression years of the present century. As the historian T.C. Smout amongst others has pointed out, seven of the Highlands and Islands counties actually reached their historic peaks of population during the first half of the nineteenth century, when the clearances were taking place. Between 1851 and 1891 there was only an 11 per cent fall in the Highlands, but an 18 per cent fall in the rest of Scotland. And in the 1880s, the massive four-volume Napier Commission report concluded that there were still too many people in the Highlands with too little land to support them. The real drain of people away from the crofts into the cities or exile took place in the years between 1851 and 1931, a period when it was virtually impossible under Scottish law to evict a Highland crofter from his holding. From a peak of just under 400,000 people in 1850 throughout the crofting counties (including Orkney and Shetland), the numbers fell to below 300,000 in the 1930s. From making up 20 per cent of the total Scottish population, the Highland proportion has dropped to barely 6 per cent today. The downward trend has more recently been reversed. There has been a growth in the population of some Highland areas, helped by modern industries such as oil, fish-farming and tourism, and by the establishment of small hi-tech businesses. The fact that today's crofter, armed with a computer, can run a second business from his front room has had a galvanizing effect on the Highlands and Islands. But it will be a long time before the number of their inhabitants reaches again its nineteenth-century pinnacles.

Arguably, the Highland economy in the nineteenth century was never a seriously viable one. The industries and crops which supported the people did so only because conditions of what today would be called poverty were accepted. As living standards rose elsewhere, in the lowlands and the cities of the mainland, so the disparity between the Highlands and the rest grew wider. Professor Smout quotes a contemporary observer, W.P. Alison, as far back as 1847, saying: 'When we find a population living chiefly on potatoes and reduced to absolute destitution, unable to purchase other food when the potato crop fails, we have at once disclosed to us the undeniable fact, that that population is redundant.' That is an extreme view, but it found an echo when a British government official, confronting the disaster of the potato famine in the 1840s, concluded: 'No resource could suggest itself more naturally, under these circumstances, than the removal of the people, bodily, from the land which is no longer adequate to support them.'

Nevertheless, the tenacity of the crofting community in sticking to the land, despite adverse conditions, has been one of its salient characteristics. 'Crofters have always considered the hardships that are the unavoidable consequences of their natural environment to be more bearable than those that have resulted from human action,' wrote Hunter. Successive governments, despite that earlier view, have therefore tried to find ways of ensuring that they could stay on the land and gain a living from it. From Gladstone's Crofters Act of 1886 to the establishment of the Highlands and Islands Development Board – later Highlands and Islands Enterprise – in 1965, there have been efforts to reverse the decline in the Highland economy, with varying degrees of success. Some imported industries, like aluminium-smelting and paper-mills, offered great hope, but fell victim to changing economic conditions. Others, like oil, brought relative prosperity and higher employment to some areas, such as those round the Cromarty Firth, in Orkney and in Shetland. But they never settled doubts about longer-term prospects. Fish-farming, probably the biggest boom industry in the Highlands, has spread rapidly around the coast, and though fears have been expressed about the pollution it can cause to the sea bed, and the way its cages detract from the unspoilt beauty of Highland sea lochs, there is no doubt that it has come to the aid of many an isolated community.

It was with these communities in mind that Scotland's biggest post-war article of reforming legislation was introduced. When the first Scottish Executive, under its First Minister, Donald Dewar, came to power in 1999, it set out to reform the way in which land in Scotland was owned and managed. The Land Reform Bill was, in one sense, an attempt to put right the wrongs of the past – or perhaps, more accurately, the perceived wrongs of the past. The Highlands was seen by some as a scar on the conscience of the nation, an area that had suffered at the hands of landowners who had been either greedy, rapacious, absent or merely indifferent. The popular image, widely held in Scotland, was of rich men of leisure, using their Highland estates as playgrounds, and preventing any development which might interfere with their sport. Far too much land, ran the argument, was concentrated in the hands of far too few people. The same families, passing on their property from generation to generation, were continuing to dominate land policy and deny the opportunity to ordinary people to have a say in the way that things should be run. At the same time, a few notorious cases were highlighted of absentee landlords who had bought land merely for tax purposes, or who had deliberately held back the economic prosperity of their estates. These 'bad apples' were constantly cited as the rationale for new legislation.

The Land Reform Act, passed in 2003, had two principal aims: to give people free access to all land. And to ensure a better distribution of the land by allowing local communities a right to buy. Thus, when a large Highland estate comes up for sale, a local community which indicates that it would like to bid for it will be given time to prepare such a bid. It may also be given financial assistance to do so. In the counties of the north, crofters will have, in addition, a pre-emptive right to buy – that is, they may buy their land even if the owner is unwilling to sell.

It is too early to say whether this law will have a wholesale effect on the way in which the Highlands are owned and managed. Opponents of the legislation point out that large investments are needed to keep a Highland estate afloat, and that, traditionally, these funds have come from outside sources provided by wealthy landowners. Where, they ask, will the resources come from to guarantee future employment? One typical 50,000 acre estate in Sutherland currently employs 15 people and costs its owner £300,000 a year. Could a local community sustain this level of investment? Meanwhile owners of salmon rivers, who also plough considerable funds into maintaining the quality of the water, protecting the fish, and ensuring that stocks remain high, argue that communities would be tempted to let out more fishing days than the river could sustain, leading to the eventual extinction of their principal source of income. By his argument, the once-vilified estate owner, far from holding back development, has become a key figure in the future of the Highlands, since it is he or she who can help maintain the balance of nature that hill-walkers and nature-lovers have come to expect. If the deer are to be kept back so that the trees can grow; if the rivers are to be protected so that the salmon thrive; if the moors are to be guarded from predators so that bird life flourishes; if all this is to be achieved, then there must be someone to employ the people to do it. And while landlords will naturally have a keen self-interest – the maintenance of a sporting estate for private pleasure or for profit – and while they may not be overjoyed by ramblers trekking across their hills, their interests and those of the naturalist often, surprisingly, combine.

As Sir Robert Grieve, first Chairman of the Highlands and Islands Development Board, once put it: 'Today, one could reasonably point out that there is the growth of an almost universal movement of ordinary folk towards the view of the sporting people of the upper classes in the last few generations; in short, the curious effect of the contemporary conservationist movement (or some interpretations of it) is to make the preservationist Highland landlord more acceptable, to urban people at least, for the first time in five or six generations.'

Sir Robert was, perhaps, a little ahead of his time. His view is countered by those who argue that allowing communities a say in how the land is run will galvanize the way that Highland land is owned and administered. It will introduce a new way of thinking about land management, give farmers the chance to diversify, and small businesses the opportunity to expand. They point to the example of the Assynt crofters, who acquired their land back in 1993, and have run it successfully ever since, and to the island communities of Eigg and Gigha where local residents, helped by considerable investments of public money, have taken over land and property and begun to develop local industries.

It is perhaps too early to say how far these developments will impact on the Highlands. Thus far there is little evidence of wholesale change. Perhaps as important in the long run will be the role of the many bodies who take an interest in the area at different levels – the Scottish Executive itself, local authorities, landowning organizations, charitable trusts, voluntary bodies, government agencies such as Scottish Natural Heritage or Highlands and Islands Enterprise, and other bodies like the Scottish National Trust and the Royal Society for the Protection of Birds, which between them own some of the most famous areas of outstanding natural beauty. Opinions vary as to how well they administer their heritage, and whether their plans for the future will work. But there has at least been recently a better awareness of the need for a co-ordinated policy. Instead of running warfare

between those who own the land and those who wish to enjoy it, an alliance, albeit an uneasy one, has begun to emerge.

That is not, of course, the only way of preserving the wild areas. Some, like the Torridon estate in Wester Ross, owned by the Scottish National Trust, are managed with visitors in mind, hill-paths carefully created and maintained, the great sandstone peaks mapped and explained to the many hundreds of enthusiasts who climb, or attempt to climb them. Others, like the Rothiemurchus estate near Aviemore, privately owned, but working closely with Scottish Natural Heritage, cater specifically for the kind of visitor who may never have climbed a hill in anger, but who still wants to see and enjoy wildlife and unspoilt country, preferably under the watchful eye of an estate ranger. Still others, like Knoydart, are relatively hard for the average tourist to reach, and cater more for the enthusiastic climber who knows the hills and is aware of the threats they face. A recent survey amongst these latter revealed that more than 70 per cent would be prepared to pay a so-called 'boot tax' – a charge paid for the privilege of climbing in certain areas. Whether schemes like this could ever be a serious source of income in the Highlands remains to be seen.

A more significant growth area has been the special category of Sites of Special Scientific Interest, given to those areas where there are rare plants, natural woodland, unspoilt tracts of moss or peatland, or other natural formations that need saving, not just from intrusive tourists, but from commercially minded estate-owners anxious to plough or plant on them. In the past large sums of money were regularly paid out in compensation to prevent that happening, with the result that large parts of the Highlands are now designated as SSSIs, with other areas falling into the lesser category of National Scenic Areas. Under European legislation, aimed at preserving particular species, such as the hen harrier, these SSSIs can become Special Protection Areas, with landowners offered management schemes to encourage them to help conserve the species. At the very least the growth in acronyms has been spectacular. Quite how successful these policies are is doubtful. Making sure the SSSIs are effectively managed and keeping an eye on them year after year is demanding, bureaucratic and expensive. It also tends to create museum pieces out of parts of our natural heritage, rather than incorporating them into the general management of the Highlands. SNH's previous chairman, Magnus Magnusson, always argued that if the voluntary principle of co-operation could be made to work, then he would like to see a time when designating bits of land in this way ceased to be necessary. So far, there is little evidence of that happening – indeed the growth of red tape has been colossal.

There will never be a consensus of view about the Highlands, about how they should look, be lived in, be nurtured or preserved. We will continue to see them through Robert Louis Stevenson's different coloured glasses – and man himself will always be a term in the equation. But at the same time we cannot simply stand back and allow these wild places to be eroded, whether by commercial exploitation, by pollution, by uncontrolled tourism or by simple neglect. Each area demands an approach geared to its particular needs. In some places tourism needs positively to be encouraged to sustain a local economy; it must, however, be sensibly and imaginatively managed rather in the way that Switzerland exploits but at the same time sustains its natural assets. In other places, there needs to be a policy of more aggressive intervention to save the land from the mass influx of people, or to control the deer population.

In the vast majority of the places revealed in these pages, the essential approach must be to find a means of balancing interests, whether those of the crofter, the laird, the tourist or the manager of local industry. There will be no magic solution, and there will be inevitable set-backs as economic trends which are more likely to have their origins in London or Brussels rather than Fort William or Ullapool have their effect. But if the lessons of the past can be absorbed and understood, and if the consistency of land management which the Highlands so desperately needs can be brought to bear, then their natural heritage stands a real chance of being saved for the future – with man playing a central role.

The first step in guarding that heritage is awareness of its value, and the photographs that follow show just how much is at stake. In taking us from the southern Highlands to the far north-west, Colin Prior and his remarkable images reveal a landscape of rare but fragile beauty which demands to be protected, cherished and renewed.

SOUTHERN HIGHLANDS

Stretching from the line of the Forth-Clyde canal across the centre of Scotland, north to the River Awe and Glen Orchy as far as the bleakness of Rannoch Moor and the grandeur of Loch Tummel, this area includes some of the best loved and most visited of all Scotland's hill country as well as some of its most remote peaks.

To the south, Ben Lomond, overlooking Loch Lomond, is the most southerly of Scotland's 'Munros' – hills over 3000 feet (914 metres) – and is the most popular and most often climbed of all the major Scottish peaks. Today, the area has been designated Scotland's first National Park, and provides well-signposted walks for even the most unpractised of visitors. But to early climbers it contained more than an element of mystery and danger, 'exciting a degree of surprise, arising almost to terror', according to an eighteenth-century account.

West from Ben Lomond, at the top of Loch Long, is the village of Arrochar, and it is north and west from here, in the mountains known as the Arrochar Alps, that some of the most popular climbing in the whole of Scotland takes place. Peaks like Ben Arthur (The Cobbler), Beinn Narnain, Beinn Ime, A'chrois, Ben Vane and Ben Vorlich are famous for their spectacular buttresses and their fearsome rock faces, coated with lichen, slippery when wet, and sufficiently challenging for some of the world's best mountaineers.

Further west, between Loch Goil and Loch Fyne, both of which reach deep into the wilds of Argyll, is Beinn an Lochain, south of the road which passes through Glen Croe and Glen Kinglas on its way to Inveraray. It is the highest mountain in the Ardgoil area, its twin peaks a mass of crags and gullies, plunging down to Loch Restil. Much of the land here is the Argyll Forest Park, managed by the Forestry Commission, and is well covered by larch and spruce with a scattering of Scots pine. The long level ridge of Binnein an Fhidhleir opens up long vistas across Loch Fyne.

The West Highland Way, which follows the east shore of Loch Lomond and takes the adventurous walker all the way to Fort William, also makes the transition from the rich green of Argyll to the hardier terrain of the western Grampians. Through Glen Falloch, it skirts the hills of Crianlarich, south-east of the town, before heading north and west. Here the hills are grass-covered and evenly weathered, the largest, like Ben More, giving superb views across half of Scotland.

Further north, through Strathfillan, woods of silver birch and some rare Caledonian pines give way to more forbidding hills and bleak moorland. The mountains here form a twisting ridge from Beinn Dorain to Beinn a'Chreachain, overlooking the West Highland railway as it snakes north to Bridge of Orchy, taking its privileged passengers through some of the most breathtaking scenery that the country's railways can offer its customers.

The rail line divides at Tyndrum, and the western spur heads for Oban, parallel with the road along Glen Lochy and underneath the great twin tops of Ben Lui, one of the grandest mountains in the southern Highlands, source of the River Tay, where Scottish Natural Heritage has established a small nature reserve, famous for its alpine plants, on the north-west side. Ben Lui lies on an almost straight east–west line between two Ben Mores – one to the east, already mentioned, and another, further off to the west, on the island of Mull, from where the whole of this jagged western coast can be seen. To the north there is the Ardnamurchan peninsula and Morvern, separated off by the deep inlet of Loch Linnhe; to the south there is Jura, Islay, the Mull of Kintyre and the Lyles of Bute.

On a bright autumn day, with the bracken golden on Ben More, Mull presents as glorious a sight as anything on Scotland's western seaboard. It is a tourist's delight, and in the summer its cottages and hotels do brisk business. But, despite the richness of its soil, Mull is sadly under-populated, its local communities diminished, its economy increasingly held back by high transport costs. Other islands, like Seil, Lung or the little slate island of Easdale, are sufficiently close to the mainland and the quarrying operations there to support a reasonable number of people, but with the decline of local farming the future prospects for these island communities are uncertain.

Left

Iceflow, Beinn an
Lochain, Glen Croe,
Argyll & Bute

Following page

Beinn Dorain and Beinn
an' Chuirn, Bridge of
Orchy, Argyll & Bute

Right

Inversnaid and Ben
Lomond, Loch Lomond,
Argyll & Bute

Following page

Erratics, Beinn Eunaich,
Glen Strae, Argyll &
Bute

Right

Cairndow, Stob an Eas,
Loch Fyne, Argyll &
Bute

Left
Binnein an Fhidhleir,
Glen Kinglas, Loch Fyne,
Argyll & Bute

Following page
Beinn Oss and Beinn
Dubhchraig from Cruach
Ardrain, Stirling District

Left
Beinn A'an and Loch
Katrine, Trossachs,
Stirling District

Following page
The Cobbler (Ben
Arthur) and Beinn Ime,
Arrochar, Argyll & Bute

Right

Kyles of Bute,
Tignabruach, Argyll &
Bute

Right

Beech and bluebells,
Bothwell, South
Lanarkshire

Left

Rowan tree, Carbeth,
Stirling District

Following page

Stob nan Eighrach,
Loch Lomond, Ardlui,
Argyll & Bute

Left

Ben More and Stob
Binnein, Strathfillan,
Stirling District

Following page

Ellanbeich, Easdale
Sound, Seil Island,
Argyll & Bute

Right

Alpenglow, Ben More
and Stob Binnein &
Cruach Ardrain, Stirling
District

Far left
The Cobbler (Ben
Arthur) and Ben Ime,
Arrochar, Argyll & Bute

Left
Winter light and cattle,
Croftamie, Stirling
District

Previous page

Ben Lomond, Inchmurrin
Island, Loch Lomond,
Stirling District

Right

The mountains of Argyll
from Cruach Ardrain,
Stirling District

Following page

Ben Lomond, Loch
Lomond, Luss, Argyll &
Bute

Left

The Devil's Poolpit,
Croftamie, Stirling
District

Right

The northward aspect
from the summit of Ben
Lomond, Stirling District

Left
Waterfall and rockpool,
Shiel Burn, An Caisteal,
Stirling District

Following page
Inveraray, from St
Catherine's, Loch Fyne,
Argyll & Bute

Previous page

Ben Lomond and Ben
Vorlich, Loch Lomond,
Argyll & Bute

Left

Loch Linnhe and the
Morvern peninsula from
Beinn a Bheithir,
Highland

CENTRAL HIGHLANDS

Rannoch Moor was once a vast pine forest. Today, bare of trees, it is a strange, bleak peatland, its dark little lochs, tussocks and boulders giving it the appearance of a lunar landscape. It is the gateway to what can loosely be described as the central Highlands, an area bounded by the Great Glen to the north and guarded by the stern peaks of Ben Alder, Schiehallion and Ben Lawers to the east.

From the south, Rannoch Moor is approached by the Black Mount and Loch Tulla, and is home to a rich variety of bird life, including dunlin and golden plover, as well as that rare plant the Rannoch rush, which is found nowhere else. This is the open prelude to the great peaks of the Glen Coe Boundary Fault, and the first sight of these daunting shapes on the horizon as you approach them from the south is always an awesome one. They rear up in the distance, gaining distinctive shapes as you get nearer, forming a fortress-wall around the southern side of the glen which was home for four centuries to the small but stubborn clan of the Glencoe MacDonalds. Its mountains, running north and west, are Buachaille Etive Beag and Buachaille Etive Mor, Beinn Fhada, Bidian nam Bian and Stob Coire nan Lochan. The tower at its summit is the top of the Crowberry Ridge, perhaps the most famous rock climb in Scotland.

These gullies and buttresses are a climber's paradise, though difficult to reconnoitre, and dangerous in poor weather. The northern wall of Glencoe, round which Colonel Hamilton brought 400 soldiers – arriving too late because of a snowstorm on the Devil's Staircase – to take his part in the massacre on the morning of 13 February 1692, is Aonach Eagach, a long and formidable ridge, whose highest peak is Meall Dearg. The rock formations of Glencoe are extraordinary, dark and red, formed of porphyritic lavas which have welled up and subsided, leaving scars and fissures like the skin on an old man's face. The glen can be grim in harsh weather, but in summer it has a gentle feel to it, with its pastureland, its waters, and its clumps of woodland reminding us that this was once a well-populated place that held clustered villages, strips of cultivated land, cattle and sheep.

To the south-west is Glen Etive, a more wooded area, where most of the Glencoe people escaped at the height of the massacre, leading down to Loch Etive and the impressive peak of Ben Cruachan. In the opposite direction, north-east, beyond the Mamore Forest, rears an even more formidable mountain, the hunched shoulder that is Ben Nevis.

This too is climbing country. Ben Nevis itself is the most walked-up mountain in Britain. The track from Achintee takes climbers up to the summit in a series of zig-zags, and can be negotiated in good weather with relative ease. But, as with so many of the high peaks of the central Highlands, it has to be treated with respect, and there are climbs on this same mountain which challenge even the most experienced mountaineers. The weather can change in minutes, from a clear day with fine views, to an impenetrable, disorientating mist, fierce winds or driving snow.

Perhaps the best introduction to the area can be gained from the West Highland Way, which runs for 95 miles (150 kilometres) from the Glasgow suburb of Milngavie through magnificent hill country to the town of Fort William on Loch Linnhe, beneath the slopes of Ben Nevis. It offers the ordinary walker a chance to admire from a distance some of the hills featured on these pages – Beinn Dorain, the Black Mount Peaks, Beinn Fhada, the Buachaille Etive Mor and many others – or venture up their slopes and commence perhaps the process of Munro-bagging: climbing the mountains of Scotland over 3000 feet (914 metres), of which there are 277. There are other routes as well, such us the Great Glen Way from Fort William to Inverness, that make full use of the old drove roads and military tracks and which follow mountain passes with dramatic names, like the Devil's Staircase, into some of the most breathtaking mountain scenery in all the Highlands.

Previous page
Lochan na h'Achlaise
and Black Mount,
Rannoch Moor, Highland

Right
Stob na Broige,
Buachaille Etive Mor,
Glen Etive, Highland

Previous page

Sron na Creise and
Buachaille Etive Mor,
Rannoch Moor, Highland

Right

Beinn Fhada and Stob
Coire nan Lochan,
Glencoe, Highland

Right

Buachaille Etive Mor
and River Coupall,
Glen Etive, Highland

Left
Buachaille Etive Mor
and River Coupall,
Glen Etive, Highland

Following page
Bidean nam Bian
and the Glencoe peaks
from Ben Starav,
Glen Etive, Highland

Left

Stob Ghabhar, Loch
Tulla, Inveroran, Argyll
& Bute

Following page

Erratic, Rannoch Moor
and Black Mount,
Highland (Autumn)

Previous page

Erratic, Rannoch Moor
and Black Mount,
Highland (Winter)

Right

Loch Ba, Rannoch Moor,
Highland

Left
Lochan na h'Achlaise
and Black Mount,
Rannoch Moor, Highland

Following page
Buachaille Etive Mor
and River Etive,
Glen Etive, Highland

Right

Stob Coire nan Lochan
and Aonach Eagach,
Glencoe, Highland

Following page

Glencoe peaks and cloud
inversion from Stob
Ghabhar, Highland

Left

Scots pine, holly and silver birch, Glen Etive, Highland

Far left
Caledonian pines,
Glen Etive, Highland

Left
Aonach Dubh and River
Coe, Glencoe, Highland

Following page
Beinn Fhada &
Buachaille Etive Mor,
Glencoe, Highland

101

Left

Lochan na h'Achlaise
and Black Mount,
Rannoch Moor, Highland

Following page

Beinn Achaladair, Beinn
an Dothaidh and Beinn
Dorain, Inveroran,
Highland

Right

Loch Ba, Rannoch Moor,

Highland

Right

Buachaille Etive Mor,
Allt nan Guibhas,
Highland

Left
Sron na Creise and River
Etive, Highland

Following page
Glas Beinn Mor and
Stob Coire an
Albannaich, Glen Etive,
Highland

Left
The Chancellor,
Aonach Eagach,
Glencoe, Highland

Following page
Beinn Toaig and Clach
Leathad, Loch Tulla,
Highland

Previous page
Buachaille Etive Mor
and River Etive, Glen
Etive, Highland

Right
Buachaille Etive Beag
and Buachaille Etive
Mor, Glen Etive,
Highland

Left

The Three Sisters,
Glencoe, Highland

EASTERN HIGHLANDS

That the Cairngorms have been proposed as a world heritage site is not surprising. They are unique in Britain, indeed in Europe, both for the open mountain wilderness they present and for the richness of their wildlife. Newly designated as a National Park, in order to conserve the fragile environment of its high peaks, this is the largest protected countryside area in Britain.

The best approach is from the south, along the A9, where, beyond Blair Atholl, the transition from the smooth hills of agricultural Perthshire to the rugged grandeur of the Grampians is sudden and spectacular. To the east, the first of the range to be seen are Beinn Dearg and Beinn a' Ghlo, part of the Atholl Forest. Then, as the road and the railway which shadows it snake deeper into Badenoch, over the Drumochter Pass at 1500 feet (458 metres), the true Cairngorms are opened up – mountains like Cairn Gorm itself, Ben MacDui and Ben Avon. To the north lie the Mondhliath Mountains, Strathspey and the Forest of Moy, but it is to the south that some of the great hill-walking areas, like Lairig Ghru, Lochnagar, Lairig an laoigh, Glenfeshie and Glen Tilt, are to be found. Often the old drove roads are muddy and eroded by the sheer weight of walking boots, yet there is a vivid sense of wildness and isolation to be experienced.

The easiest access is probably from Aviemore, striking east by Loch Morlich to the foothills of Cairngorm; Glenmore Lodge is a favourite departure point, and it was from here that the late Eric Beard set up something of a record by climbing the four highest Cairngorms, and arriving back at the lodge in four and a half hours; another approach, via the A93 north to Braemar, takes the walker to the Spittal of Glenshee, a delight for climbers and skiers alike; there are easier walks further east, up Glen Esk to Tarfside and towards Lochnagar.

Some estates, like Rothiemurchus and Mar Lodge, are managed with walkers and tourists in mind. Some, like Atholl, Invercauld and Braemar, are sporting estates. Others, like Abernethy Forest, owned by the Royal Society for the Protection of Birds, and the St Cyrus Nature Reserve, towards the eastern coast, are conserved for wildlife. The range of vegetation, alpine and sub-alpine, pine forests and birch wood, heath and grassland, is vast, supporting a wide variety of animal and bird life. Rivers like the Feshie, the Spey, the Ythan, the Avon, the North Esk and the Dee provide spectacular scenery and equally spectacular sport.

The Cairngorms will always present a challenge for conservationists. Their wildness is their greatest asset, but at the same time they have to be protected from the many tourists and hill-climbers who visit the area in growing numbers. A balance must also be struck between those who need to make a living in the area, perhaps from deer-stalking or grouse-shooting, and the requirements of the conservationists who want to control deer numbers and regenerate woodland. Progress has been made, though it is slow and patchy, but at least these days the two sides talk to each other. The great test over the next 20 years will be the new Cairngorm National Park, which attempts to reconcile all these conflicting interests. Whether it can strike the balance between man and nature that previous regimes have failed to achieve remains to be seen.

The eastern Highlands are not all cliffs and soaring mountains. In one image, Colin shows us a glimpse of a Highland glen in autumn. This stretch of the River Dee, running through a broad valley near Braemar, with Lochnagar in the distance, is typical of this part of the country. Study it closely and you can see some of the contrasts that combine to give the Highlands their singular charm. Although it is still a wild place, it is gentle; much of the Highlands are like that – broad sweeps of country, tree-clad for the most part, where rivers run their course as quietly and as slowly as if they were crossing an English meadow.

Speyside, famous for its whisky and its salmon fishing, is also a place of rare beauty, to be explored on foot and enjoyed at close quarters. The trees here are beech and birch, the colours golden, the autumn rain soft and caressing. The waters that cross from west to east run into large estuaries of sandy beach, rich in bird life, strung out along the coast of Moray, Nairn, Banff and Aberdeenshire. Often the Highlands are pictured as wild and desolate, their hills dour, their rivers roaring in spate: yet here, on the North Esk, the Dee, the Don or the Spey is that gentler part of the Highlands which complements the rich drama of the high peaks.

Left

Derry Cairngorm and
Loch Etchachan,
Cairngorms, Highland

Following page

Geal Charn and
A' Chailleach,
Monadhliath Mountains,
Newtonmore, Highland

Left
Rothiemurchus Forest,
Loch an Eilein, Glen
Feshie, Highland

Following page
Castle Hill, Loch
Morlich, Highland

Right

River Bran,
The Hermitage, Dunkeld,
Perth & Kinross

Left
Boulders & moss,
Glen Esk, Angus

Right

St Cyrus Nature Reserve,
Aberdeenshire

Left

Braeriach and Lairig Ghru, Rothiemurchus Forest, Highland

Following page

Beinn Mheadhoin and Stacan Dubha, Loch Avon, Cairngorms, Highland

Left
River North Esk,
Glen Esk, Angus

Far left
River North Esk in
spate, Glen Esk, Angus

Left
Metamorphic rocks,
River Tromie, Strathspey,
Highland

Right

A'Mharconaich and
An Torc, Pass of
Drumochter, Highland

Following page

Ebb tide, St Cyrus
Nature Reserve,
Aberdeenshire

Left

Lochnagar and White
Mounth, River Dee,
Braemar, Aberdeenshire

Following page

Sunset, Glen Feshie,
Highland

Far left
Thistle and bumblebee,
Dunkeld, Perth &
Kinross

Left
Common mallows and
meadowsweet,
St Cyrus Nature Reserve,
Aberdeenshire

Following page
Sands of Forvie, Ythan
Estuary, Newburgh,
Aberdeenshire

Left
Castle Hill, Loch
Morlich, Highland

Following page
Derry Cairngorm and
Beinn Mheadhoin,
Cairngorms, Highlands

Right

Meall a' Buachaille,
Rothiemurchus Forest,
Cairngorms, Highland

Far left
Salmon bothy and nets,
St Cyrus Nature Reserve,
Aberdeenshire

Left
River North Esk,
Glen Esk, Edzell, Angus

Left

River North Esk and the
Rocks of Solitude, Angus

Left

River North Esk and the
Rocks of Solitude, Angus

NORTH-WEST HIGHLANDS

If a highland wilderness can be said truly to exist, then this is it. Running from the hills of Sutherland and Wester Ross down to the Great Glen, it is, for some, the spiritual centre of the Highlands. Certainly, poets like Norman MacCaig and Sorley Maclean, naturalists like Frank Fraser Darling, or writers like Gavin Maxwell, have cherished the north-western Highlands above all others: 'Nowhere in all the west Highlands and Islands have I seen a place of so intense and varied beauty in so small a compass,' wrote Maxwell of his beloved Sandaig.

There is no better way of starting than taking the train from Dingwall to Kyle of Lochalsh, from the rich farmland of Easter Ross, through moor and mountain country of rare beauty, clattering past tiny stations like Achnasheen, following the course, first of the River Bran, then the River Carron, until the sea opens up and the Cuillin Hills become the middle ground of the most heart-wrenching view in Scotland. To the south, there are peaks which anyone can climb,

around Glen Shiel and Kintail – the Five Sisters, The Saddle, Beinn Fhada, Beinn Sgritheall, Faochag – and sea-bays of shimmering beauty – Morar, Arisaig, Glenelg, Inverie – where even today you can walk, undisturbed by anything other than a questioning seal. To the north, beyond the Applecross peninsula, lies Loch Torridon, with its hills of strange Torridonian sandstone, weathered and heroic. The heights of Liathach and Beinn Eighe are much-loved by climbers, but it is still possible, even in midsummer and however crowded the car-parks, to find yourself alone within minutes as you strike out for some distant corrie. Torridon is owned by the National Trust for Scotland, which maintains its paths well. Further north, at Loch Maree, Scottish Natural Heritage takes over, equally meticulous in its care.

If you have chosen to drive from the east, rather than go by rail, you approach Loch Maree by Kinlochewe, opening up a sudden view to the west, with Beinn Eighe to the left, Slioch to the right, and in front of you the loch, the sea and distant Harris. It is as unexpected as it is spectacular. The road west to Gairloch now takes the motorist past the head of Loch Ewe, then circles back on itself, until it is running east past Gruinard Bay, down Little Loch Broom and under the magnificent escarpment of An Teallach – 'Liathach's only rival', according to the mountaineer Tom Weir. Looking east from here, across the Dundonnel Forest, there is another peak, Beinn Dearg. Frank Fraser Darling wrote of this:

When the snow is down, an east wind blowing hard, the sky leaden and the tops partly hidden, Beinn Dearg and An Teallach roar to one another from the unapproachable country of their summits. I do not know what causes this deep song in the hills … I am inclined to place (it) in the same category of sounds as the phenomenon of the singing sands.

North again, past the prosperous tourist and fishing town of Ullapool, and Sutherland takes over. The mountains of Suilven, Stac Pollaidh, Canisp, Quinag, and Ben More Assynt, are so distinctive, so full of unexpected shape and character, that you can never weary of them. They have, as Tom Weir puts it, 'a dignity out of all proportion to their size'. Glacier-formed, they were once covered by pine forest, and remnants can be seen on the island in the middle of Loch Assynt, where the sheep could not get at it. Further north still, past the villages of Scourie and Kinlochbervie – the latter a successful fishing port – the hills have names like Arkle and Foinaven, familiar to the turf, for this is land owned by the Westminster estates and the Duchess named her horses after her mountains. Bending round Loch Eriboll, the road runs east to Tongue and thence to Thurso. Here, the last of the Sutherland hills, Ben Hope and Ben Loyal, look down over the great flatness of the Caithness moorland. There is little sign of habitation amongst these rolling acres, save for the occasional mound of abandoned stones, a bothy or a boathouse.

Previous page

Slioch, Letterewe Forest,
Loch Maree, Highland

Right

Traigh Allt Chailgeag,
Loch Eriboll, Durness,
Highland

Following page

Liathach and Loch Clair,
Glen Torridon, Highland

Previous page
Suilven, Cur Mor and
Stac Pollaidh, Enard
Bay, Highland

Right
River Shiel, Glen Shiel,
Kintail, Highland

Left
River Moriston, Glen
Moriston, Highland

Following page
Isle Martin, Loch
Broom, Ardmair,
Highland

Left
Beinn Ghoblach,
Gruinard Bay, Laide,
Highland

Following page
Forcan Ridge,
The Saddle from
Sgurr na Sgine,
Glenshiel, Highland

Right

Loch Osgaig, Stac
Pollaidh and Ben More
Coigach, Highland

Right

Hill burn and rowan,
Glen Affric, Highland

Left
Silver birch and Scots
pine, Glen Affric,
Highland

Left
Oldshoremore Bay,
Kinlochbervie, Highland

Following page
Beinn Dearg, Beinn
Eighe and Liathach from
Beinn Alligin, Highland

Left

Ben an Eoin, Stac
Pollaidh, Inverpolly
Nature Reserve,
Highland

Following page

An Teallach: Sgurr
Fiona, Lord Berkeley's
Seat, Dundonnell,
Highland

Right

Hoar frost and silver birch, River Merkland, Highland

Far right

Carn Mairi, Barrisdale Bay, Loch Hourn, Knoydart, Highland

Following page

Loch Beinn a Mheadhoin, Fasknakyle Forest, Glen Affric, Highland

Previous page

Sgurr na Ciste Duibhe,
Sgurr na Carnach and
Sgurr Fhuaran, Kintail,
Highland

Right

Sandwood Bay and
Sandwood Loch,
Highland

Following page

Beinn Dearg Mor, Beinn
Dearg Bheag, Loch na
Sealga, Fisherfield
Forest, Highland

Right

Snow and rocks,

River Glascarnoch,

Garve, Highland

Left

Waterfall, River Shiel,
Glen Shiel, Kintail,
Highland

Following page

Liathach and Loch Clair,
Glen Torridon, Highland

Right

Beinn Sgritheall,
Loch Hourn, Knoydart,
Highland

Following page

Boulder field, Slioch,
Letterewe Forest,
Loch Maree, Highland

Previous page
Sgurr na Ciste Duibhe
and Saileag from
Faochag, Kintail,
Highland

Right
Caledonian pine, Glen
Affric, Highland

Left
Cul Beag and Stac
Pollaidh, Inverpolly
Nature Reserve,
Highland

Following page
Beinn Alligin, Upper
Loch Torridon, Highland

Previous page
Suilven, Inverpolly
Nature Reserve,
Highland

Right
River Bran, Strath Bran
Forest, Highland

THE ISLANDS

'Not to know the islands,' said Hugh MacDiarmid, 'is like having a blunt sensation in the tip of your fingers.' There cannot be many travellers in the Hebrides who would disagree. This journey takes us from the Butt of Lewis in the north to the Sound of Gigha in the south, and in between there is an enormous variety of geology, vegetation, animal life – and social conditions. Ownership is perhaps an even more burning issue here than elsewhere in the Highlands, because to maintain an island economy requires consistency and dedication, and many of the maverick purchasers who have decided down the years that owning an island would be fun, or a shrewd investment, are short of both. Depopulation is still the greatest threat to the islands. Here, man does not affect his surroundings because of the weight of his numbers, but because of a lack of them.

Lewis is the northern part of a double island, the largest in Britain, with Harris as its southern end. The basic rock of which it is formed is ancient, and over the years it has been ice-worn into domes and ridges, with deep valleys and fjords on the east, and long stretches of sand and machair on the west. 'This is the oldest land in Europe,' wrote Compton Mackenzie, '… the hills of Harris have been so long above the sea as to make parvenus of the Alps.' The highest peak is the Clisham in Harris, which is over 2600 feet (795 metres). Though the waters of the Minch have been fished to destruction over the years, the town of Stornoway is still an important port, and while crofting these days is a border-line activity, it is still widely practised throughout the island, as is the weaving which produces the famous Harris tweed. This is peat country, and the deposits all over the island can be as deep as 15 feet (4.5 metres), producing a fuel which compares well with coal in its output of thermal energy. Many thousands of acres have been successfully converted to grassland. Harris, by contrast, is an island of lochs and mountains, wildly beautiful, a mecca for tourists and anglers, but with a less resilient economy than Lewis. A recent buy-out by local crofters of one of its largest estates will be something of a test-case for the principles of Land Reform. The island of Scalpay to the south, supports a fishing community, and yet further south, Berneray, which is close to the shore of North Uist, is also thriving.

North Uist is the most northerly of a pendant of islands, with

Benbecula, south Uist and Barra its southern string. It is a long, low-lying island, with hills to the north and east and a mass of lochs in the interior. There is a nature reserve owned by the RSPB which is home to the rare red-necked phalarope and many other species including the corncrake and the corn bunting. Benbecula, the stepping-stone between North and South Uist, is connected by bridge and causeway to both islands, so there is now a through route from Pollachar in South Uist to Berneray in the north. The airport on Benbecula is an equally important economic and social lifeline. South Uist has the characteristic west-coast sand and machair, with high hills down its spine, and boggy moorland on the eastern side. Its three long sea-lochs, Skiport, Eynort and Boisdale, almost sever it.

Finally, Barra is the most westerly inhabited island in Great Britain, and certainly one of the most beautiful, with great cliffs and sandy bays, wild moorland and long stretches of machair, the sandy flatlands which support a profusion of flowers in the spring. As with the remainder of the Outer Hebrides, remoteness – and the weather – have been the great protectors against the erosion of mass tourism. The number of visitors grows steadily, but these are still islands where solitude can be easily guaranteed – all too easily, in the eyes of some.

The same cannot be said of Skye, lying some 15 miles (24 kilometres) to the east, and a magnet for the modern tourist. Visitors numbers have increased significantly since the opening of the Skye Bridge which, for the first time, connects island to mainland. The 24 rock peaks of the Cuillin Hills are constantly climbed by experts and amateurs alike, and seem hardy enough to resist the worst of the erosion to be found elsewhere. The hills of Trotternish, to the north, and the island of Raasay to the east, with its rich soil and its lush grassland, are still places to be explored in peace, and in the south-west corner, to walk by Loch Scavaig to Loch Coruisk, round the bay of Camusunary, is an act of relative solitude. Most visitors prefer the eastern route, from Broadford north to Portree, whose harbour is a delight. Some will go on to view the astonishing rock outcrop of the old Man of Storr just north of Portree. Further on, past the little crofting township of Staffin, is the Quiraing, a dramatic canyon of grey rock and black pinnacles, with a table of flat turf on top. The western spur of road, which divides at Sligachan in the heart of Skye, takes one to Dunvegan, seat of the Macleods of Macleod, and on to Waternish.

To the south of Skye, Rum, now a nature reserve, is a mountainous island of red Torridon sandstone, with a plunging coastline, and several peaks over 2000 feet (6096 metres), the highest being Askival at 2652 feet (808 metres). It must always have been a difficult island to farm, and it has had a history of emigration and depopulation. The great exodus of its people took place in 1826 when about 400 of the inhabitants emigrated to America, leaving fewer than 130 people behind. The island was turned over to a herd of 8000 sheep which steadily transformed the vegetation of the island. Today it is inhabited only by employees of Scottish Natural Heritage – it was acquired by SNH's predecessor, the Nature Conservancy, in 1957. There are golden eagles, a herd of some 1500 red deer, a small colony of wild goats, and the famous wild Rum ponies. Close study of the deer has shown a deterioration in their quality since sheep and cattle were removed from the island. The lack of manuring and the coarsening of the grass appear to have had a severe effect on the grazing. However, the study of an island deprived of a viable population has yielded valuable information about how to restore a vegetation which has suffered from over-grazing and burning.

Canna, to the west of Rum, a green and fertile island, was once the herring centre of the Hebrides, its natural harbour offering shelter to hundreds of vessels. More recently it has seen its population fall to a level which at present is fewer than twelve. It has owed its survival as an island crofted in the traditional manner to the enlightened ownership of Dr John Lorne Campbell, whose knowledge of Gaelic language and culture is legendary. It was well tended over the 43 years that he and his wife owned it, with dykes maintained, ditches dug and trees planted. In 1981 it was gifted to the Scottish National Trust whose task it is now to ensure that Canna has a viable future.

To the south-east of Canna, beyond Rum, lies Eigg with its distinctive Scuir standing out like a natural sphinx, overlooking 7000 acres of relatively low ground. It became the property of Yorkshire-born Keith Shellenberg, a controversial landowner, who attempted to improve conditions on the island but did not endear himself to the local inhabitants. Finally, he sold it to the islanders themselves, who are now attempting to restore its fortunes. The tiny island of Muck, to the south of Eigg, has three families on it, with the redoubtable McEwans of Muck still making a living there.

South to Mull, Coll and Tiree, three islands of differing fortunes and geology. Mull is volcanic, with its highest peak, Ben More, standing at 3170 feet (966 metres). In the south, at Carsaig, there is a very

English-looking chalk-stream with watercress – one of only two in the Highlands. Elsewhere the ground is more rugged. Despite the fact that it is relatively rich agriculturally, Mull's indigenous population has fallen over the years to fewer than 2000, though in summer its cottages are let and tourists throng the place. The holy island of Iona to the south-west is a strong attraction for visitors. Coll, to the east, is low-lying, its highest peak no more than 340 feet (104 metres), with fine sandy beaches and good grazing on the machair. It supports a farming rather than a crofting community, since in the last century, Ayrshire farmers were asked to take over the land after a clearance, but its present population is only about 150. Tiree is even flatter, but is a place of great charm and beauty, with silver beaches and green grassland.

Jura, to the south, means, in Gaelic, 'deer island' and it has had a long history as a place for hunting. In the southern part of the island the Paps of Jura rise to 2571 feet (784 metres), from where, on a good day, you can see from the Cuillin in the north to the Isle of Man in the south. The west of the island is wild, trackless and devoid of human habitation. Elsewhere, crofting and a newly built distillery support a population of around 250 people. Perhaps the most famous physical feature of Jura is the fearsome tidal race of Corriebhreacan, running between Jura and the island of Scarba. It is officially deemed unnavigable, with a speed of eight knots and only fifteen minutes of slack water time.

Islay is the largest island of the Inner Hebrides, a place of green, arable land and peat, used to prepare its famous malt whiskies. Its three main townships support a population of around 4000, and though its proximity to Glasgow has meant a steady drain of people away from the island over the years, the balance of tourism, farming and distilling, together with smaller local industries, has made Islay a reasonably settled place. Less stable, in recent years, has been Gigha, which lies between Islay and the Mull of Kintyre. Here, for years, Sir James Horlick, of malted milk fame, attended to a small but contented population of around 190 people. He encouraged dairy farming, created a superb garden of rhododendrons, and encouraged the introduction of regular water and electricity supplies. Later, after several changes of ownership, the future became less certain. Then, in 2004, a resourceful group of islanders banded together to buy Gigha for themselves. The hope now is that Gigha at least has discovered one vital element in the battle for survival – a dedicated and active community. The fragile economy of the Hebrides will always need protection, whether it is lobbying for better transport links, campaigning for grants, or seeing that the interests of crofters or fishermen are properly represented in council chambers, in Edinburgh or at Westminster.

Left
Loch Dubh, Isle of Islay,
Argyll & Bute

Following page
Saligo Bay, Isle of Islay,
Argyll & Bute

Left

Ben More and Eorsa
Island, Loch na Keal,
Isle of Mull,
Argyll & Bute

Following page

Lichens and boulder,
Ben More, Isle of Mull,
Argyll & Bute

Right

Paps of Jura from
Foreland, Isle of Islay,
Argyll & Bute

Left
Ben Hiant,
Ardnamurchan,
Sound of Mull,
Isle of Mull,
Argyll & Bute

Following page
Ardnamurchan Point
from Mishnish,
Isle of Mull,
Argyll & Bute

Previous page
Sea spray and basalt,
Isle of Staffa,
Argyll & Bute

Right
Marsco and Beinn Dearg
Mhor, Broadford Bay,
Isle of Skye, Highland

Previous page

Old Man of Storr and
satellites, Isle of Skye,
Highland

Right

Bla Bheinn and Gharb
Bheinn, Loch Slapin,
Isle of Skye, Highland

Left

The Cuillin, Loch
Scavaig, Isle of Skye,
Highland

Following page

Sgurr nan Gillean, Black
Cuillin, Isle of Skye
Highland

Right

Sgurr an Fheadain,
Bidean Druim nan Ramh,
Coire na Creiche, Isle of
Skye, Highland

Following page

The Quiraing, Trotternish
Ridge, from The Storr,
Isle of Skye, Highland

Previous page
Beinn Sgritheall and
Ladhar Beinn, Loch
Hourn, Sound of Sleat,
Isle of Skye, Highland

Right
Traigh Nisabost, Sound
of Taransay, Isle of
Harris, Western Isles

Left
Bla Bheinn and Clach
Glas, Cuillins, Isle of
Skye, Highland

Following page
The Cuillin, Loch
Scavaig, Isle of Skye,
Highland

Left

The Storr, Trotternish
Ridge, Isle of Skye,
Highland

Following page

Sron Scourst and
Uisgnaval Mor, Forest of
Harris, Isle of Harris,
Western Isles

Left
Traigh Nisabost, Sound
of Taransay, Isle of
Harris, Western Isles

Right
Bioda Bhuidhe and the
Totternish Ridge, The
Quiraing, Isle of Skye,
Highland

Left
Waterfall, Allt Coire
nam Bruadaran, Marsco,
Isle of Skye, Highland

Following page
Cleiseval and Uisgnaval
Mor, Traigh Rosamol,
Isle of Harris,
Western Isles

Left
Traigh Luskentyre and
Corran Seilebost, Isle of
Harris, Western Isles

Following page
Isle of Taransay, Traigh
Seilebost, Isle of Harris,
Western Isles

Previous page
Loch na Cleavag,
Cravadale, Isle of Harris,
Western Isles

Right
Boulder and lichens,
Elgol, Isle of Skye,
Highland

Left

Loch Airigh na
h'Achlais, Loch
Druidibeag Nature
Reserve, South Uist,
Western Isles

Northern Scotland

The locations of
photographs in the book
are identified by page
number on these maps

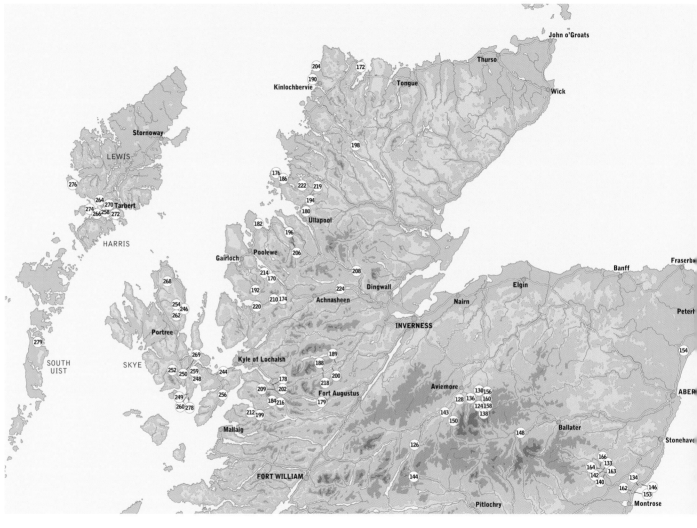

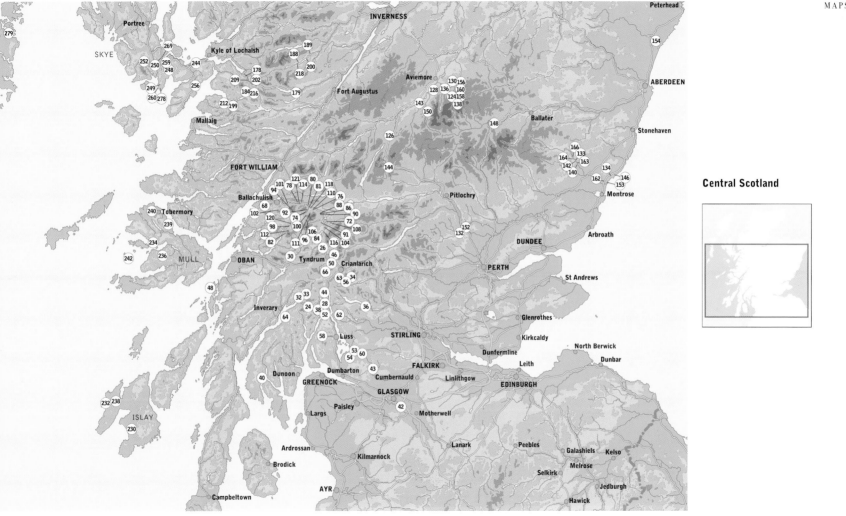

Central Scotland

CAPTURING THE INVISIBLE ESSENCE

During the past ten years whilst speaking at lectures and workshops people have often come up to talk about their own experiences and dilemmas. Many would say to me 'I'm only an amateur' as if apologizing in advance for their predicament. For the record, I don't differentiate between the two groups and see the only difference being that professionals make their living from photography whilst amateurs don't.

In many respects, amateur photographers can be at a considerable advantage if they organize their lives outside their professions to capitalize on photographic opportunities, free of the need to make a financial return. The great irony is that often the mechanics of making a living as a professional gets between you and your desire to create new work, and this can be a constant source of frustration.

Over the years, I have seen many examples of fine nature photography produced by amateur photographers, simply because some of them have discovered their inner paths. They create intimate photographs with an emotional connection with the elements of the natural world. This I would add, does not apply to all amateurs across the board but it is true of some individuals. The key to producing competent photography, day after day, year after year, is to discover an internal path and stay on it.

Conversely, I have seen examples by working professionals that are nothing more than impartial records of the natural world with a poor range of visual clues. Professionals are, on the whole, guilty of not taking pictures for themselves, and fill their lives fulfilling other people's dreams instead of their own. Many are simply completing their next assignment and have in fact nothing to say about the world around them. It has always been my belief that the development of one's own work is the path to self-fulfilment. Regardless of their status, what sets good photographers apart is their individual vision. If they are able to consistently produce photographs that have a distinctive 'thumbprint' they have probably embarked on an inner path.

For me, it took some time to recognise what I was pursuing, and the irony was that it was invisible. The ultimate challenge is to photograph something, which in reality, doesn't exist. It is of course the essence – that quality which constitutes or marks the true nature of anything, which often eludes the photographer. The location and composition are of great importance but they alone will not produce success. Other factors including the quality of light, the balance of shadow and light, textural qualities and, of course, experiences are all ingredients in the equation. But ultimately, it is the way in which the eye and brain interpret the image which will determine whether a mental leap is made to another plane, or if the image remains mundane. One thing is certain; success is uncertain and can never be guaranteed.

A great image leaps off the light box – if you have to ask yourself 'Do I think I've got the picture?', then you haven't. There's no real formula to guarantee results besides experience, which certainly enhances the number of occasions on which you will capture that seen in the mind's eye.

Another question that I'm often asked is 'Which came first, mountaineering or photography?' The answer is neither – I found photography as a means by which I could express a passion for the natural world. Apart from the sheer pleasure of climbing mountains, there are some basic reasons for being on or around the summits at dusk and dawn. Firstly from an elevated viewpoint the scale and character of the landscape is revealed. Secondly you're at the point where light first strikes. We've all been in deep glens at dawn and marvelled at the pink light illuminating the clouds and the mountaintops. Shooting from the roadside across a loch towards the peaks will probably show a difference of about three stops between the sunlit peaks and the loch, revealing a composition where one fifth of the image is illuminated by the magic dawn light, whilst four-fifths are in shadow.

On the summit however, somewhat cooler I might add, this surreal pink light is at your feet. You compose a corniced ridge in the foreground glistening in this rare light against the angular peaks of the surrounding cirque of mountains. Deep below in the glens a dark loch can be seen from which a river drains, giving contrast to the awesome scene. Did I capture the elusive essence? It's processes like this – in which I pre-visualize an image, perhaps years before – that encourage success when I finally manage to capture it on film. And it is this endless search for the Holy Grail which drives me out again and again and prompts the answer to another question which I'm often asked – ' What is your best photograph?' – to which I reply, 'Always the one I've yet to take!'

NOTES ON THE PHOTOGRAPHS

This photographic portfolio has been compiled over a period of 20 years and includes many of my early images along with some of my most recent. I have used a number of cameras and one lesson I have drawn is that there is not a single camera which will do it all. Photography is just like everything else in life, you don't get something for nothing.

Top-end 35mm cameras such as the Canon EOS1V with a combination of their professional L type lenses produce superb quality transparencies from a relatively small camera, capable of capturing a fleeting moment in nature. Beyond this, medium-format cameras use 120 roll film to yield larger areas of exposed film that in turn will give better reproduction, due to the smaller magnification required from the film. The price to be paid is in greater camera weight, slower lenses and less response – although cameras such as the Hasselblad H1 have interfaces not dissimilar to 35mm cameras and feature auto focus, multi-segment metering and motor drives. Panoramic cameras fall into the same category and, although electronically unsophisticated, remain fast and responsive, yielding four 6x17 transparencies from a single 120 roll film.

Finally, large-format view cameras yield transparencies that are 5x4 inches in proportion and give the ultimate in photographic quality (larger formats of 5x7 and 10x8 are available but fall outside my working experience). Reproductions from transparencies this size result in extremely high resolution and colour reproduction – often you feel as if you could touch a texture or smell the landscape when presented with a fine art print reproduced from a 5x4 transparency. However, these cameras are heavy, bulky and extremely slow to use and for all they can deliver in terms of quality, I find that they can get between you and the subject. Instead of feeding off what's happening 'out there', one becomes a slave to the technical disciplines which the camera demands.

At the time of writing, digital capture has been evolving at a rapid pace and we now have cameras such as the Canon EOS1Ds that has a full-frame 35mm, 11.1 megapixel sensor, which yields images with the equivalent resolution of a medium-format 6x7 transparency. For the first time, in essence, we are getting more for less – more quality for less weight and bulk, which remains the greatest limiting factor for outdoor photography. Similarly with medium format, digital backs designed to interface with cameras such as the Hasselblad H1 are capable of delivering a 132Mb file from a 22-megapixel sensor, which will render the use of large-format cameras redundant and confine them to the display cabinet.

Digital has become the common language for image capture and unless it is embraced, you can't be part of the conversation. With it will come new challenges in refining it to capture the subtleties and nuances of the natural world, and in the comprehension of topics such as white balance and colour spaces. One thing is certain: the value of being able to review captured images in real time on location. Frequently, images are rejected because we failed to recognise at the time the significance of a shadow or the inclusion of a tree at the edge of the frame that proves confusing.

I have made the first steps in purchasing a Canon1Ds and I plan to explore the world of medium-format digital photography and the new opportunities for image capture, for publication in a future book.

The photographs published here are all produced from scanned transparencies in a variety of formats, as described in the data relating to each thumbnail. Over the years I have used Nikon's, Canon's, a variety of Hasselblad's, a Mamiya RZ67, a Fuji 6x8, a number of Linhof 617's, a Linhof 612PCII, Fuji GX617S and a variety of 5x4's including Linhof's, Arca Swiss 6x9 and 5x4 and an Ebony. What have I learnt? That being a photographer is not good for the lower back! In photographic terms, experiment with cameras until you find a format that suits the way you would see the world. I have always maintained that the 35mm format with a 3:2 ratio is well suited to landscape photography in general, and is capable of producing distinctive upright and landscape images.

Weight remains the biggest consideration when getting to a remote location – there's a limit to how much equipment you can carry if you plan to photograph mountains and it's surprising how a little weight can drastically reduce your performance. Add to the equation ice axe, crampons, tent, stove, sleeping bag and food and you'll be stretching for the same multi-vitamin leg pills that the coyote used to catch the road-runner, albeit unsuccessfully, as I recall. When I started out as a professional, the advice an old press photographer gave me was that you could shoot the majority of assignments with two lenses, a 35mm and an 85, and could add a 24mm. This still remains the case although these focal lengths are now absorbed into zooms. My advice is to carry as little as is required to achieve your objective and to immerse yourselves in the experience of being outdoors. It should be the experience of being outdoors that validates your photography and not the reverse.

All images are shot on Fuji Velvia with the use of a Gitzo Mountaineer tripod.

COLIN PRIOR 2004

pages 24–25
Iceflow, Beinn an Lochain, Glen Croe, Argyll & Bute
Camera: Linhof 617S;
Lens: Schneider Super-Angulon 90mm f5.6
This was my first ever panoramic photograph. So keen was I, having just taken delivery of the first re-designed Linhof 617S in the UK, that I departed in poor weather for a relatively close mountain. These icicles were taken on the steep east face, which rises above Loch Restill.

pages 26–27
Beinn Dorain and Beinn an' Chuirn, Bridge of Orchy, Argyll & Bute
Camera: Linhof 617S;
Lens: Schneider Super-Angulon 90mm f5.6
Rising out of Tyndrum, Beinn Dorain looks awesome on first sight from the road – its scale seems to defy logic, its summit rising from an apron of steep slopes at an angle of 45°. Photographed here at dawn, spindrift blew off the summit as the sun illuminated the shoulder.

pages 28–29
Inversnaid and Ben Lomond, Loch Lomond, Argyll & Bute
Camera: Linhof 617S;
Lens: Schneider Super-Angulon 90mm f5.6
This image was taken from Inveruglas, now part of Loch Lomond National Park, before tourist developments took place. Looking south towards Ben Lomond, the sunrise was spectacular, creating hues of crimson and yellow. The challenge is to retain the spiritual essence of the area, which has inspired for generations, without turning it into a theme park.

pages 30–31
Erratics, Beinn Eunaich, Glen Strae, Argyll & Bute
Camera: Linhof 617S;
Lens: Schneider Super-Angulon 90mm f5.6
Deposited as the glacier receded, these erratics would have been bound within the ice and may have been responsible for cutting and scraping the landscape as the glacier moved. Photographed on the southern side of the Dalmally horseshoe en route to Stob Diamh and Ben Cruachan.

page 32
Cairndow, Stob an Eas, Loch Fyne, Argyll & Bute
Camera: Hasselblad SWC;
Lens: Zeiss Biogon 38mm f4.5
The village of Cairndow photographed from the northern shore of Loch Fyne before salmon farming was established. The scene was very still, and as smoke rose from a fire in the distance the light enveloped the landscape with a painterly quality, reminiscent of the Dutch school.

page 33
Binnein an Fhidhleir, Glen Kinglas, Loch Fyne, Argyll & Bute
Camera: Hasselblad 503CX;
Lens: Zeiss Distagon CF 50mm f4
Although at first glance there may seem to be little that is unusual in this image, consider that Loch Fyne is a sea loch and that sea water normally freezes at –10°C, and you might agree that this is a rare photograph. The influence of freshwater run-off which lies on the surface will have been a factor.

pages 34–35
Beinn Oss and Beinn Dubhchraig from Cruach Ardrain, Stirling District
Camera: Linhof 617S;
Lens: Schneider Super-Angulon 90mm f5.6
Setting off at 6.30am under a thick blanket of cloud, I eventually pushed through it on Grey Heights, where the cloud lay below me in the glen. As the sun rose and began to illuminate the opposite mountain tops, this sea of mist swirled below like a tidal race until it finally dispersed into the atmosphere.

pages 36–37
Beinn A'an and Loch Katrine, Trossachs, Stirling District
Camera: Fuji GX617; Lens: SWD90mm f5.6
Although one of the smallest hills in the Trossachs, Beinn A'an has a surprisingly lofty viewpoint with excellent views west across Loch Katrine to the Cobbler and Beinn Narnain. I waited on the summit that evening to witness a spectacular sunset and then in the darkness got lost in the forest.

pages 38–39
**The Cobbler (Ben Arthur) and Beinn Ime,
Arrochar, Argyll & Bute**
Camera: Fuji GX617; Lens: W180mm f6.7
Having spent years trying to find the ultimate image
of the Cobbler, I had climbed Ben Reoch on the
opposite of Loch Long and shot with a large
telephoto but still was not satisfied with the
extended foreground. This image was shot from a
hovering helicopter, the only one in the book, and
finally gave me the result I had sought for years.

pages 40–41
Kyles of Bute, Tignabruach, Argyll & Bute
*Camera: Linhof 617S;
Lens: Schneider Super-Angulon 90mm f5.6*
Before the advent of interchangeable lenses on
panoramic cameras, the 90mm was permanently
mounted on the camera. Now with the Fuji GX617, I
have the choice of 90,180 and 300mm lenses. I
would now have used the 300mm to focus in the
centre of this image where the main interest is,
effectively cropping out the expansive shadow areas.

page 42
**Beech and bluebells, Bothwell,
South Lanarkshire**
*Camera: Hasselblad 503CX;
Lens: Zeiss Sonnar CF 150mm f4*
For a couple of weeks each year in early May, the
landscape undergoes a rejuvenation. Trees explode
into leaf and the profusion of greens signal growth.
This simple image captures the essence of this time,
as a beech tree's leaves come to life like the wings
of a butterfly.

page 43
Rowan tree, Carbeth, Stirling District
Camera: Nikon F4; Lens: AF80-200 f2.8ED
I came upon this rowan tree on a hillside and
visualized an image which separated the tree from
the hillside in a single plane. I chose to use the
200mm end of the zoom and selected the relatively
wide aperture of f4, which gave the desired result I
envisaged.

pages 44–45
**Stob nan Eighrach, Loch Lomond,
Ardlui, Argyll & Bute**
Camera: Fuji GX617; Lens: SWD90mm f5.6
Near the head of Loch Lomond at Stuckendroin,
the stands of oaks and birches which line the side
of the loch give way, and unobstructed views to the
east side are possible. From here the tiny croft at
Doune is visible, lying on the path of the West
Highland Way.

pages 46–47
**Ben More and Stob Binnein, Strathfillan,
Stirling District**
*Camera: Linhof 617S;
Lens: Schneider Super-Angulon 90mm f5.6*
Intent on capturing the Crianlarich group of
mountains, which comprise Ben More, Stob Binnein
and Cruach Ardrain (visible), I desperately searched
for a suitable foreground as the sun began to drop.
By sheer luck, I found this rock formation, which
mimicked the distant mountains.

pages 48–49
**Ellanbeich, Easdale Sound, Seil Island,
Argyll & Bute**
*Camera: Linhof 617S;
Lens: Schneider Super-Angulon 90mm f5.6*
Gale-force winds batter the coastline in Easdale
Sound where in November 1881 huge waves swept
over the entire island and completely flooded the
slate quarries. At their peak during the 19th
century Easdale quarries were producing 9 million
slates annually.

pages 50–51
**Alpenglow, Ben More and Stob Binnein
and Cruach Ardrain, Stirling District**
*Camera: Linhof 617S;
Lens: Schneider Super-Angulon 90mm f5.6*
Alpenglow comes about because of the double
journey light must take through atmospheric haze.
Light rays pass once from the sun to ground level
and then they must continue through additional
haze back up from the horizon to reach a
mountaintop after sunset. The double journey
doubles the light's redness.

page 52
**The Cobbler (Ben Arthur) and Beinn Ime,
Arrochar, Argyll & Bute**
Camera: Arca Swiss F Metric 6x9;
Lens: Schneider Apo-Symmar 210 f5.6
Officially know as Ben Arthur, the name 'The
Cobbler' was used by local people as early as 1799
in its Gaelic form An Greasaiche Crom, meaning
'The Crooked Shoemaker' – likening the rock on the
north top to a cobbler bowed over his work.

page 53
**Winter light and cattle, Croftamie,
Stirling District**
Camera: Hasselblad 503CX;
Lens: Zeiss Distagon CF 50mm f4
This was one of my early photographs with a
Hasselblad, which I chose to hand-hold at 250th at
f5.6 in an effort to capture the cattle. There's
something about the image I like, in particular the
sharp foreground and the fact that the cattle are
soft and out of focus. It has, in a strange way, the
painterly feel of a Constable landscape.

pages 54–55
**Ben Lomond, Inchmurrin Island,
Loch Lomond, Stirling District**
Camera: Fuji GX617; Lens: EBC Fujinon T300 f8
As cold air from the surrounding landmass comes in
contact with the warmer water, mist forms above
the surface of the Loch, captured here at dawn from
Duncryne. While the sun began to light up the
landscape, skeins of pink-footed geese broke
formation and landed in the fields on the loch-side,
their distinctive wink-wink ung-ung sounds
resounding in the air.

pages 56–57
**The mountains of Argyll from Cruach Ardrain,
Stirling District**
Camera: Linhof 617S;
Lens: Schneider Super-Angulon 90mm f5.6
The view north-west towards the peaks of Glencoe
from the summit of Cruach Ardrain which sits
amidst the Crianlarich group. Although the summit
lies some distance in from the starting point, it is an
exhilarating walk up the mountain's spine and is my
personal favourite of the group.

pages 58–59
**Ben Lomond, Loch Lomond, Luss,
Argyll & Bute**
Camera: Fuji GX617; Lens: W180mm f6.7
Having spent a number of trips exploring the ridges
high above Loch Lomond, I finally found a point on
Beinn Dubh from which I felt Ben Lomond could be
seen at its best. After two unsuccessful attempts, I
finally captured this image at dawn in late October
when the autumn colours were at their finest.

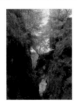

pages 60–61
**The Devil's Poolpit, Croftamie,
Stirling District**
Camera: Linhof 617S;
Lens: Schneider Super-Angulon 90mm f5.6
Photographed from the foot of the gorge which
forms the pulpit, with walls of red sandstone rising
some 80ft (25m) to the top. Over the centuries the
river has eroded the soft sandstone to create this
spectacular fissure, winding its way almost invisibly
through dense woodland.

page 62
**The northward aspect from the summit of
Ben Lomond, Stirling District**
Camera: Nikon F2AS; Lens: Nikkor 28mm f2.8
One of my early photographs, taken on 31 December
1979. I am happy to report that little has changed
on the top! However, the same cannot be said of the
area in general and I am astonished by the
commercial developments that have taken place
since I shot this image.

page 63
**Waterfall and rock pool, Shiel Burn,
An Caisteal, Stirling District**
Camera: Ebony 45SU;
Lens: Schneider APO Symmar 180mm f5.6
I was drawn to this waterfall – smoothed and
polished by the passage of time – by the intricate
patterns and detail. The use of a large-format 5x4
camera makes it possible to record the subtle detail,
which can be reproduced in print with the same
clarity as I originally observed.

pages 64–65
Inveraray, from St Catherine's, Loch Fyne, Argyll & Bute
Camera: Linhof 617S;
Lens: Schneider Super-Angulon 90mm f5.6
This was the first time that I had witnessed a sea-loch freezing, probably about fifteen years ago. Given the mildness of our winters now, I doubt if there have been many instances in recent times when this phenomenon could have occurred.

pages 66–67
Ben Lomond and Ben Vorlich, Loch Lomond, Argyll & Bute
Camera: Fuji GX617; Lens: SWD90mm f5.6
A rather unusual perspective of Loch Lomond, looking south from the lower slopes of Beinn Dubhchraig. To the west of Ben Lomond, the distinctive peaks of Ben Vorlich, and the Arrochar Alps, Ben Vane, Beinn Ime and Beinn Narnain can be seen.

pages 68–69
Loch Linnhe and the Morvern peninsula from Beinn a Bheithir, Highland
Camera: Linhof 617S;
Lens: Schneider Super-Angulon 90mm f5.6
Rising gracefully above the narrows of Loch Leven at Ballachulish, Beinn a Bheithir (Hill of the Thunderbolt) is formed by two peaks on a long curving ridge. Photographed from Sgorr Dhonuill, the view south-west encompasses the islands of Shuna and Lismore.

pages 72–73
Lochan na h'Achlaise and Black Mount, Rannoch Moor, Highland
Camera: Linhof 617S;
Lens: Schneider Super-Angulon 90mm f5.6
Each time I visit this location it is different. Many of the large boulders, which exist in a semi-submerged state, have become a lesson in impermanence. Photographed here at dawn, the water reflects the last cold light of night as the mountains are illuminated with the warm light of morning.

pages 74–75
Stob na Broige, Buachaille Etive Mor, Glen Etive, Highland
Camera: Linhof 617S;
Lens: Schneider Super-Angulon 90mm f5.6
Although the Buachaille Etive Mor appears to stand in solitary isolation at the head of Glen Etive, it is in fact linked by a high-level traverse with three other recognised tops. Photographed in swirling mist from Stob na Doire, Stob na Broige lies at the end of the ridge and is preceded by Stob Coire Altruim.

pages 76–77
Sron na Creise and Buachaille Etive Mor, Rannoch Moor, Highland
Camera: Linhof 617S;
Lens: Schneider Super-Angulon 90mm f5.6
A combination of fine light, technical competence and personal vision are the essential components required to create a quality photograph. The initial act of visualizing a meaningful photograph has more in common with meditation than with any professional skill.

pages 78–79
Beinn Fhada and Stob Coire nan Lochan, Glencoe, Highland
Camera: Linhof 617S;
Lens: Schneider Super-Angulon 90mm f5.6
High above Glencoe from the slopes of Am Bodach, the summit of Stob Coire nan Lochan stands behind the ridge of Beinn Fhada. Whilst winter conditions can produce the greatest drama, the sun is never high enough to illuminate the interior of the glen until late April – this image was shot in June.

page 80
Buachaille Etive Mor and River Coupall, Glen Etive, Highland
Camera: Canon EOS1V; Lens: TS-E 24mm f3.5
There are few days in a year when conditions such as these present themselves. For many years I had attempted to shoot this image without success. Either the frost had stripped off the birch leaves or the wind blew the foliage, blurring the image. However this morning in October 2003 provided the perfect conditions.

page 81
Buachaille Etive Mor and River Coupall,
Glen Etive, Highland
Camera: Arca Swiss F Metric 6x9;
Lens: Schneider Super-Angulon XL 58mm f5.6
I arrived at this well know location at dawn to find
four photographers already in place. It was a classic
sunrise with clouds turning pink and light slowly
moving down the mountain. All foreground areas
were in shadow, the image being very one-
dimensional and I waited for the sun to illuminate
the foreground by which time all other
photographers had long departed.

pages 82–83
Bidean nam Bian and the Glencoe peaks from
Ben Starav, Glen Etive, Highland
Camera: Linhof 617S;
Lens: Schneider Super-Angulon 90mm f5.6
This remains without doubt my signature image.
Rarely do photographs like this happen, becoming a
conduit for my own most powerful emotional
response. Without that response a photograph is less
than the scene it depicts – a two dimensional
representation with a greatly impoverished range of
visual clues.

pages 84–85
Stob Ghabhar, Loch Tulla, Inveroran,
Argyll & Bute
Camera: Linhof 617S;
Lens: Schneider Super-Angulon 90mm f5.6
Near Inveroran on the south side of Loch Tulla is
one of the few original stands of Scots pine,
overlooking Coire na Muic on Stob Ghabhar.
Photographed in early September as the bracken
begins to change into an autumnal palette, the
silence was pierced only by the enigmatic sound of
little grebes.

pages 86–87
Erratic, Rannoch Moor and Black Mount,
Highland (Autumn)
Camera: Linhof 617S;
Lens: Schneider Super-Angulon 90mm f5.6
The Rannoch Moor has all the classic features of
glacial deposition – Lochan na h'Achlaise and Loch
Ba were both created as the glaciers receded.
Erratics are deposited in large quantities around the
lochs and give scale to the tremendous Coire Ba
captured behind.

pages 88–89
Erratic, Rannoch Moor and Black Mount,
Highland (Winter)
Camera: Linhof 617S;
Lens: Schneider Super-Angulon 90mm f5.6
Under a thick blanket of snow the landscape assumes
a very different character and a new challenge for
the photographer. As with any landscape which is
predominantly one colour, like the dense greens of
mid August, it is difficult to find contrasting features
to create interest. A dusting of snow as seen overleaf
is far preferable to a dump!

page 90
Loch Ba, Rannoch Moor, Highland
Camera: Arca Swiss F Metric 5x4;
Lens: Schneider Apo-Symmar 210 f5.6
These ancient rocks are a constant source of
fascination for me – a silent measure of time, sitting
undisturbed throughout the centuries. Ironically, at
one stage in their existence they would have been
caught up in an ice sheet in a state of motion, albeit
a slow one.

page 91
Lochan na h'Achlaise and Black Mount,
Rannoch Moor, Highland
Camera: Arca Swiss F Metric 5x4;
Lens: Schneider Super-Angulon 90mm f5.6
Despite its bulk, weight and lack of speed, the view
camera remains a unique tool. Its ability to render
sharpness from foreground through to infinity by
employing tilt is addictive and can be seen in this
example. The size of the transparency also helps
record the minutest subtlety and detail.

pages 92–93
Buachaille Etive Mor and River Etive,
Glen Etive, Highland
Camera: Linhof 617S;
Lens: Schneider Super-Angulon 90mm f5.6
Standing at the entrance to Glencoe, the Buachaille
Etive Mor has become an icon of the Scottish
Highlands. Seen from the road, its mass and
angularity epitomize the very essence of the ancient
Highland landscape. This is Scotland seen at its best.

pages 94–95
Stob Coire nan Lochan and Aonach Eagach, Glencoe, Highland
Camera: Linhof 617S;
Lens: Schneider Super-Angulon 90mm f5.6
Photographed from the summit of Bidean nam Bian as the last rays of light skimmed the summit of Stob Coire nan Lochan. Beyond the Pinnacles and the Aonach Eagach Ridge on the north side of Glencoe, Ben Nevis and the Mamores can be seen. The following morning rain arrived and these unique conditions disappeared.

pages 96–97
Glencoe peaks and cloud inversion from Stob Ghabhar, Highland
Camera: Linhof 617S;
Lens: Schneider Super-Angulon 90mm f5.6
Having started off in the early morning under a thick blanket of mist we pushed through the canopy at around 2000ft (650m) into a bright clear day. Beneath, the cloud lay like an inland sea, creating islands from the peaks of Glencoe and beyond. The conditions prevailed all day with no wind affecting the inversion.

pages 98–99
Scots pine, holly and silver birch, Glen Etive, Highland
Camera: Linhof 617S;
Lens: Schneider Super-Angulon 90mm f5.6
Tumbling down the mountain-side, the water has polished flumes into the metamorphic rock with precision. Sustained by stream-fed nutrients, these trees have survived in the face of adversity, and will in turn help sustain wildlife – redwings were feeding on the holly berries as we approached.

page 100
Caledonian pines, Glen Etive, Highland
Camera: Arca Swiss F Metric 6x9;
Lens: Schneider Apo-Symmar 210 f5.6
Although the Forestry Commission only fenced off this area a few years ago, there has already been significant regrowth of broad-leaved trees. Birch, rowan and sapling Scots pine have been re-introduced to rejuvenate the original stands and all are prospering in the absence of red deer. Controlling the deer's numbers is an important part of the re-afforestation equation.

page 101
Aonach Dubh and River Coe, Glencoe, Highland
Camera: Nikon F2AS; Lens: Nikkor 28mm f2.8
Draining through Loch Achtriochtan, the River Coe continues its journey east to Loch Leven. Rising at the head of Glencoe, it is probably most visible in spate, at the Meeting of Three Waters in the Pass. I chose to polarize this image to separate the clouds in from the sky.

pages 102–103
Beinn Fhada and Buachaille Etive Mor, Glencoe, Highland
Camera: Linhof 617S;
Lens: Schneider Super-Angulon 90mm f5.6
The view east at sunset, overlooking the Buachaille Etive Beag and Buachaille Etive Mor and across the Rannoch Moor to Schiehallion. To the south the distinctive conical top of Stob Binnien in the Crianlarich group is visible. The horizontal visibility that evening was superb.

pages 104–105
Lochan na h'Achlaise and Black Mount, Rannoch Moor, Highland
Camera: Linhof 617S;
Lens: Schneider Super-Angulon 90mm f5.6
A good photograph depends on balance, both in terms of composition and in light and shadow. For this image to work successfully, I let the sun rise in order to illuminate the mountains and the foreground, without which the image would have been overwhelmed by shadow and have negative connotations.

pages 106–107
Beinn Achaladair, Beinn an Dothaidh and Beinn Dorain, Inveroran, Highland
Camera: Linhof 617S;
Lens: Schneider Super-Angulon 90mm f5.6
Standing above the east shore of Loch Tulla, these three mountains along with Beinn a' Chreachain form part of the Great Wall of Rannoch, the boundary between the old Pictish Kingdom of Alba to the east and the Dalriadic Kingdom of the Scots in the west.

pages 108–109
Loch Ba, Rannoch Moor, Highland
Camera: Linhof 617S;
Lens: Schneider Super-Angulon 90mm f5.6
Punctuated by numerous lochans, the Rannoch Moor
is an important breeding ground for a wide variety
of birds, including black and red-throated divers,
little grebe, and greenshank. Apart from the small
islands in the lochans, which are well wooded with
birch, rowan and pine, the moor is treeless due to
the deer population.

page 110
Buachaille Etive Mor, Allt nan Guibhas,
Highland
Camera: Ebony 45SU;
Lens: Schneider Super-Angulon XL 90mm f5.6
In this study of the Buachaille, the summits of Stob
Dearg and Stob na Doire are both visible. Two other
tops not visible are also recognized on the ridge,
Stob Coire Altruim and Stob na Broige, which give
superb views into Glencoe.

page 111
Sron na Creise and River Etive, Highland
Camera: Ebony 45SU;
Lens: Schneider Super-Angulon XL 90mm f5.6
Falling in a series of waterfalls, the River Etive has
carved a series of spectacular pools in its journey
towards Loch Etive. Rising in the Black Corries of
the Rannoch Moor, its waters exhibit a peaty tinge
when compared with the clear water of the River
Coe. Photographed on a cold December morning,
during which I waited for mist to clear the
mountaintops.

pages 112–113
Glas Beinn Mor and Stob Coire an Albannaich,
Glen Etive, Highland
Camera: Linhof 617S;
Lens: Schneider Super-Angulon 90mm f5.6
On the summit of Ben Starav, I lingered to capture
the last rays of light as they fell on the peaks of Glen
Coe. Further to the east, the Beinn Dorain group can
be seen across Loch Tulla and Stob Ghabhar. As I
shot these images, I watched two ptarmigan, that had
turned golden in the magic light.

pages 114–115
The Chancellor, Aonach Eagach, Glencoe,
Highland
Camera: Linhof 617S;
Lens: Schneider Super-Angulon 90mm f5.6
Photographed from the summit of Am Bodach.
Below is the exposed rock outcrop known as the
Chancellor, from which airy views can be
experienced. The main ridge walk includes two
Munros, Meall Dearg and Sgorr nam Fiannaidh.
However, the traverse itself offers few great photo
opportunities.

pages 116–117
Beinn Toaig and Clach Leathad,
Loch Tulla, Highland
Camera: Linhof 617S;
Lens: Schneider Super-Angulon 90mm f5.6
Now a scene of tranquility, Loch Tulla is an example
of an ice-dammed loch which was formed during the
later stages of de-glaciation of the Rannoch Moor
area. The absence of any breeze allowed me to
capture the reflection clearly with the relatively long
shutter speed of 1 second at f22.

pages 118–119
Buachaille Etive Mor and River Etive,
Glen Etive, Highland
Camera: Linhof 617S;
Lens: Schneider Super-Angulon 90mm f5.6
Representing a height of experience in Scottish
mountaineering, the Buachaille Etive Mor attracts
superlatives. Captured here at dawn, it is one of the
few mountains that are sufficiently distinctive to be
instantly recognisable.

page 120
Buachaille Etive Beag and Buachaille
Etive Mor, Glen Etive, Highland
Camera: Hasselblad 500CM;
Lens: Zeiss Distagon CF 50mm f4
Photographed at dusk from the south shore of the
nameless lochan in Glen Etive, the two Buachailles
stand like giant sentinels at the head of the glen. As
the sun dropped, the mountains began to reflect
crimson hues on the mountain-tops by which time the
foreground and island were completely in shadow.

page 121
The Three Sisters, Glencoe, Highland
Camera: Canon EOS1N;
Lens: EF 28-70 f2.8L USM
Dominating the south side of the glen are the Three
Sisters of Glencoe, which are essentially outlying
spurs of the region's highest mountain, Bidean nam
Bian. Photographed here in early March are two of
the three, Gearr Aonach and Aonach Dubh. The
third, Beinn Fhada, lies to the left of the Hidden
Valley.

pages 124–125
**Derry Cairngorm and Loch Etchachan,
Cairngorms, Highland**
Camera: Linhof 617S;
Lens: Schneider Super-Angulon 90mm f5.6
Composed predominantly of granite, the high
Arctic plateau of the Cairngorms contains five
summits over 4000ft (1220m), the highest of which
is Ben Macdui at 4295ft (1309m). On this occasion,
I had to work quickly as the ascending sun
threatened to flare my lens.

pages 126–127
**Geal Charn and A' Chailleach, Monadhliath
Mountains, Newtonmore, Highland**
Camera: Linhof 617S;
Lens: Schneider Super-Angulon 90mm f5.6
Despite their lack of dramatic features, the
Monadhliath Mountains give a sense of wildness and
remoteness. I took this photograph from the south
as the weather began to clear, and watched a golden
eagle spiralling in the circotherms in the sky above.

pages 128–129
**Rothiemurchus Forest, Loch an Eilein,
Glen Feshie, Highland**
Camera: Fuji GX617; Lens: SWD90mm f5.6
Across Loch an Eilein on the western flanks of Creag
Fhiaclach the treeline reaches 2130ft (650m), the
highest in the Cairngorms. This image shot at dawn
shows the autumn landscape at its best, before frosts
begin to cut the leaves from the trees.

pages 130–131
Castle Hill, Loch Morlich, Highland
Camera: Fuji GX617; Lens: SWD90mm f5.6
Loch Morlich is a classic example of a 'kettle hole' –
a water-filled depression that marks the final resting
place of a massive fragment of ice. The fragment
became embedded in gravel and sand, forming a
cavity that filled with water as the ice thawed.

page 132
**River Bran, The Hermitage, Dunkeld,
Perth & Kinross**
Camera: Ebony 45SU;
Lens: Schneider Super-Angulon XL 90mm f5.6
I was drawn to this particular rock, its surface
smoothed in places by centuries of water erosion
and etched elsewhere with lichens and mosses.
I applied back tilt to my view camera to keep
everything from the foreground rock to the
waterfall in sharp focus. The latent detail
recorded on the transparency is superb.

page 133
Boulders and moss, Glen Esk, Angus
Camera: Ebony 45SU;
Lens: Schneider Super-Angulon XL 90mm f5.6
In late March the landscape's vibrancy tends to be
muted by the ravages of winter, so when I found this
vivid green moss cover on rocks, it became the
subject of an image. I always find it a challenge to
find pattern in chaos – it's like finding a world
within a world.

pages 134–135
St Cyrus Nature Reserve, Aberdeenshire
Camera: Linhof 617S;
Lens: Schneider Super-Angulon 90mm f5.6
The coastal strip between the River North Esk
estuary and the rocky headland, backed by sea cliffs
creates a wide variety of habitats for wildlife.
However, in recent years populations of herring
gulls, fulmars and terns have diminished as a direct
effect of sea pollutants. Photographed at dawn, the
cliffs turned an orange hue as the tide flooded.

pages 136–137
**Braeriach and Lairig Ghru,
Rothiemurchus Forest, Highland**
Camera: Linhof 617S;
Lens: Schneider Super-Angulon 90mm f5.6
Cutting through the heart of the Cairngorms, the
Lairig Ghru is a spectacular mountain pass that
climbs to a height of 2756ft (840m) with the
massive bulk of Ben Macdui 4290ft (1309m) to the
east, and Braeriach 4250ft (1296m) and Cairn Toul
4233ft (1291m) to the west. The old drove road
linked Braemar with Aviemore.

pages 138–139
**Beinn Mheadhoin and Stacan Dubha, Loch
Avon, Cairngorms, Highland**
Camera: Linhof 617S;
Lens: Schneider Super-Angulon 90mm f5.6
Overlooking the deep glacial chasm that hosts Loch
Avon gave an immense feeling of exhilaration and
of vastness. I truly felt a tiny part of this giant
landscape and vulnerable – there is an inherent
fear of how easily one could be engulfed on this
Arctic plateau.

pages 140–141
River North Esk, Glen Esk, Angus
Camera: Linhof 617S;
Lens: Schneider Super-Angulon 90mm f5.6
Rising in Loch Lee, the River Esk cuts its way
through rock clefts, forming deep river pools and
waterfalls of white torrents. In other stretches, a
more sluggish river laps over tiny beaches of gravelly
white sand, where dippers dart from rock to rock.

page 142
**River North Esk in spate,
Glen Esk, Angus**
Camera: Arca Swiss F Metric 6x9;
Lens: Schneider Apo-Symmar 210 f5.6
After five days of torrential rain, the river had risen
13ft (4m) and was frothing its way downstream
through the narrows. As the ambient light was low, I
chose a 10-second exposure in an effort to capture
the movement of the water and to absorb the vivid
foliage colours.

page 143
**Metamorphic rocks, River Tromie, Strathspey,
Highland**
Camera: Hasselblad 503CX;
Lens: Zeiss Sonnar CF 150mm f4
Rising in Loch Bhrodainn, which in turn drains into
Loch an t-Seilich, the River Tromie flows through a
series of metamorphic rocks. A band of quartz
diagonally cuts through this section, which was what
originally drew me to the composition. The colour
harmony and the wispy water offer a soft contrast to
the angularity of the rocks.

pages 144–145
**A'Mharconaich and An Torc,
Pass of Drumochter, Highland**
Camera: Linhof 617S;
Lens: Schneider Super-Angulon 90mm f5.6
The temperature was –10°C when I photographed this
at dawn. I exposed the image before dropping down
into the mist-filled glen. At first the freezing mist was
too dense, but as the sun began to rise, a rare white
rainbow formed – a full white arc composed of ice
particles which are unable to refract the spectrum of
light into the colours of a rainbow.

pages 146–147
**Ebb tide, St Cyrus Nature Reserve,
Aberdeenshire**
Camera: Fuji GX617; Lens: SWD90mm f5.6
The late February sun rose into an initially clear
sky before a weather front approached from the
west. As cloud thickened, it created a moody
atmosphere, and while the sun struggled to break
through I managed to shoot four frames before it
deteriorated irreversibly.

pages 148–149
**Lochnagar and White Mounth, River Dee,
Braemar, Aberdeenshire**
Camera: Linhof 617S;
Lens: Schneider Super-Angulon 90mm f5.6
Rising high in the Cairngorms, the River Dee flows
some 90 miles (145km) to the sea at Aberdeen. Its
source, at the Wells of Dee, is very close to that of
the River Avon. The middle reaches between Ballater
and Banchory boast some of the finest salmon beats
on the river. Names like Cambus o May, Dinnet and
Glentanar will be familiar names even to those who
have only dreamed of fishing there.

pages 150–151
Sunset, Glen Feshie, Highland
Camera: Linhof 617S;
Lens: Schneider Super-Angulon 90mm f5.6
Characterized by openness and wildness, a complex
mix of heather moorland, farmland and woodland
can be found in Glen Feshie and the surrounding
areas. Fragments of the Caledonian pine forests
are home to a variety of animal species, including
pine martins, red squirrels, wildcats, crested tits
and capercallie.

page 152
**Thistle and bumblebee, Dunkeld,
Perth & Kinross**
Camera: Nikon F4;
Lens: Micro-Nikkor 60mm f2.8
I was drawn to this scene during a walk through
farmland by the presence of the bumblebee on the
thistle – without which I wouldn't have felt
compelled to photograph it. In a strange way the bee
tells a story about the interconnectedness of the
natural world.

page 153
**Common mallows and meadowsweet,
St Cyrus Nature Reserve, Aberdeenshire**
Camera: Nikon F2AS; Lens: Nikkor 180 f2.8ED
Whilst photographing shelducks on the North Esk
estuary, these rim-lit wildflowers caught my attention
and I patiently waited for the wind to drop before
photographing them. Shelducks (not in frame) are
distinctive with a dark green head, with black, white
and chestnut body plumage.

pages 154–155
**Sands of Forvie, Ythan Estuary, Newburgh,
Aberdeenshire**
Camera: Linhof 617S;
Lens: Schneider Super-Angulon 90mm f5.6
The Sands of Forvie are an outstanding beach-dune
complex that has developed over the last 4000
years, forming one of the largest areas of blown
sand in Scotland. As the Scottish glaciers melted
approximately 10,000 years ago, vast quantities of
sediment were transported by rivers to the coast
where they were deposited.

pages 156–157
Castle Hill, Loch Morlich, Highland
Camera: Linhof 617S;
Lens: Schneider Super-Angulon 90mm f5.6
Matched only by Baffin Island and Labrador, the
Cairngorms offer a plethora of glacial and post-
glacial landforms. The rolling granite plateau is
broken by deep glaciated glens and impressive
corries sheltering high lochans, whilst Loch Morlich
provides an example of a 'kettle-hole' formed as the
glacier melted.

pages 158–159
**Derry Cairngorm and Beinn Mheadhoin,
Cairngorms, Highland**
Camera: Linhof 617S;
Lens: Schneider Super-Angulon 90mm f5.6
The elevated plateau of the Cairngorms has created
an environment that is essentially Arctic in nature,
reflected in the landscape, soils, vegetation and
wildlife. This fact, combined with the effects of
global warming, could potentially push species such
as the ptarmigan and mountain hare to the edge of
extinction.

pages 160–161
**Meall a' Buachaille, Rothiemurchus Forest,
Cairngorms, Highland**
Camera: Linhof 617S;
Lens: Schneider Super-Angulon 90mm f5.6
Following a bitterly cold morning with temperatures
of –12°C, the sun rose to illuminate pine trees
glistening with hoar frost. Beyond, the summit of
Meall a' Buachaille (Hill of the Herdsman) is visible,
from which a path descends to the Ryvoan bothy and
An Lochan Uaine.

page 162
**Salmon bothy and nets, St Cyrus Nature
Reserve, Aberdeenshire**
Camera: Nikon F2AS; Lens: Nikkor 28mm f2.8
One of my early images of the salmon bothies when
they were still in operation. Between St Cyrus and
Montrose, large-scale netting took place at static
sites along the beach and salmon heading for the
North Esk estuary were harvested in great numbers.
I am delighted that I had the opportunity to record
this way of life before it vanished.

page 163
River North Esk, Glen Esk, Edzell, Angus
Camera: Nikon F2AS; Lens: Nikkor 24mm f2.8
This varied and beautiful river is renowned for excellent salmon, sea trout and brown trout fishing. Salmon are expected at the beginning of the season from the lowest pools at Kinnaber to the Loups at Gannochy, upstream of Edzell.

pages 164–165
River North Esk and the Rocks of Solitude, Angus
Linhof 612PCII;
Lens: Schneider Super-Angulon 65mm f5.6
Photographed in a deep cleft that I consider one of the most dramatic sections of the river. A combination of lichen-covered rock faces, a blend of beech, birch and rowan trees and a potent river provide the raw material for powerful imagery.

pages 166–167
River North Esk and the Rocks of Solitude, Angus
Linhof 612PCII;
Lens: Schneider Super-Angulon 65mm f5.6
In this section of the river, the trees on the opposite bank are more prominent. Illuminated by a low sun, I particularly liked the way the light picked out the rowan tree and also the way the leaves have created colour in the rock ledges, reminiscent of an Andy Goldsworthy creation.

pages 170–171
Slioch, Letterewe Forest, Loch Maree, Highland
Camera: Fuji GX617; Lens: SWD90mm f5.6
Photographed during a spectacular five-day period of weather in mid October 2003. I had attempted for four years to capture this image without success. Finally, the right conditions prevailed, and I used a polarizer to separate the clouds from the blue sky. Loch Maree is an area of outstanding beauty that has not been degraded by developments.

pages 172–173
Traigh Allt Chailgeag, Loch Eriboll, Durness, Highland
Camera: Fuji GX617; Lens: W180mm f6.7
In a break between two weather fronts, the winter light transforms the landscape. Unlike the surrounding strata, which are of Torridonian sandstone, the coastline of Durness is composed of Cambrian limestone, continually eroded by the sea.

pages 174–175
Liathach and Loch Clair, Glen Torridon, Highland
Camera: Fuji GX617; Lens: SWD90mm f5.6
Due to their proximity to the sea, the Torridon Giants are always a challenge to photograph, with climatic conditions which change rapidly. Ironically, this very unpredictability can manifest itself in spectacular events such as this sunrise.

pages 176–177
Suilven, Cur Mor and Stac Pollaidh, Enard Bay, Highland
Camera: Fuji GX617; Lens: SWD90mm f5.6
Photographed as a seascape, the hills of Assynt can be seen in a different, yet relevant context. The sea cliffs to the west of the bay support a large colony of shags, and peregrines can be seen heeling over the stacks and sending sea birds into panic.

page 178
River Shiel, Glen Shiel, Kintail, Highland
Camera: Ebony 45SU;
Lens: Schneider Super-Angulon XL 90mm f5.6
Encrusted in a thick frost, these river boulders had an intangible quality that I was keen to capture. Using rear tilt on the view camera, I was able to bring their crystalline texture into sharp focus whilst retaining sharp focus on the distant mountains.

page 179
River Moriston, Glen Moriston, Highland
Camera: Ebony 45SU;
Lens: Schneider Super-Angulon XL 90mm f5.6
Sub-zero temperatures and a high moisture content
in the air can lead to a heavy coating of frost.
Birch trees are transformed into ghostly translucent
skeletons, separated from the landscape. When the
sun rises, it is literally possible to watch the tree
materialize as the ice melts.

pages 180–181
Isle Martin, Loch Broom, Ardmair, Highland
Camera: Fuji GX617; Lens: EBC Fujinon T300 f8
Isle Martin, presently uninhabited, is situated at the
mouth of Loch Broom some 3 miles (5km) north-
west of Ullapool, Wester Ross. The only specific, but
anecdotal, references are to a Saint Martin who is
reputed to have established a monastery there
probably around AD 300–400 and from whom the
island takes its name.

pages 182–183
**Beinn Ghoblach, Gruinard Bay,
Laide, Highland**
Camera: Linhof 617S;
Lens: Schneider Super-Angulon 90mm f5.6
An inlet on the coast of Wester Ross, Gruinard Bay
lies between Loch Ewe and Little Loch Broom. It
receives the Gruinard and Little Gruinard rivers
and contains Gruinard Island, once involved in the
development of biological warfare.

pages 184–185
**Forcan Ridge, The Saddle from
Sgurr na Sgine, Glenshiel, Highland**
Camera: Linhof 617S;
Lens: Schneider Super-Angulon 90mm f5.6
The traverse of the Saddle by the Forcan Ridge
followed by Sgurr na Sgine and Foachag is one of
the best expeditions in Kintail. Photographed here
as the sun was setting, we watched two golden
eagles soaring around the peaks which intensified
the experience of being in such a wild place.

pages 186–187
**Loch Osgaig, Stac Pollaidh and
Ben More Coigach, Highland**
Camera: Fuji GX617; Lens: SWD90mm f5.6
At the end of a chain of freshwater lochs that cuts
through the heart of Coigach, Loch Osgaig lies in a
great fold between Ben More Coigach and the
mountains of Inverpolly. Photographed at dusk, as
the sun dropped behind the Rubha Mor peninsula.

page 188
Hill burn and rowan, Glen Affric, Highland
Camera: Hasselblad 503CX;
Lens: Zeiss Sonnar CF 150mm f4
Rowan berries are eaten by a variety of birds in the
forest. Fieldfares and redwings time their migrations
from Scandinavia to the UK to coincide with the
availability of rowan berries. In the process, they
will disperse the seeds, thereby enabling a new
generation of young rowans to grow.

page 189
**Silver birch and Scots pine, Glen Affric,
Highland**
Camera: Hasselblad 503CX;
Lens: Zeiss Sonnar CF 150mm f4
One of the largest ancient Caledonian pinewoods is
in Glen Affric, home to a number of unique species,
including crossbills, crested tits, black grouse and
capercallie. Red, roe and sike deer are all present
and can be seen more often in the winter.

pages 190–191
Oldshoremore Bay, Kinlochbervie, Highland
Camera: Linhof 617S;
Lens: Schneider Super-Angulon 90mm f5.6
Beyond Kinlochbervie at Oldshoremore lies one of
the finest sandy bays in Sutherland. Surrounded by
broad marram dunes punctuated with harebells, red
clover, buttercup and dandelion, the sands attract
oystercatchers and dunlin. Photographed here in the
early morning at low tide.

pages 192–193
Beinn Dearg, Beinn Eighe and Liathach from Beinn Alligin, Highland
Camera: Fuji GX617; Lens: SWD90mm f5.6
Amidst perfect conditions, the last rays of light illuminate Beinn Dearg and Beinn Eighe. Shooting as quickly as I was able, I captured the drama while the light faded from the foreground. Minutes later I was back on the summit shooting Baosbheinn with a 180mm lens in a distinctly red light.

pages 194–195
Ben an Eoin, Stac Pollaidh, Inverpolly Nature Reserve, Highland
Camera: Linhof 617S;
Lens: Schneider Super-Angulon 90mm f5.6
Rising at an angle of 45° the weathered sandstone slopes of Stac Pollaidh have intrigued onlookers for centuries. Separated from the Ben More Coigach range by Loch Lurgainn, the entire area has an 'ancient' feel. Photographed on a very still, early morning.

pages 196–197
An Teallach: Sgurr Fiona, Lord Berkeley's Seat, Dundonnell, Highland
Camera: Fuji GX617; Lens: SWD90mm f5.6
Illuminated by the dawn sun, the Torridonian sandstone gives off a red glow, explaining its name An Teallach, meaning 'The Forge'. The weathered turrets and towers that rise above Loch Toll an Lochain include no fewer than ten tops over 3000ft (914m).

page 198
Hoar frost and silver birch, River Merkland, Highland
Camera: Arca Swiss F Metric 6x9;
Lens: Schneider Apo-Symmar 210 f5.6
In ambient temperatures of −8°C, a freezing fog blowing off Loch Merkland had covered the foliage along the river with a thick hoar frost. As the sun rose I witnessed, for the second time only, a rare white rainbow – composed of ice crystals unable to refract into a spectrum.

page 199
Carn Mairi, Barrisdale Bay, Loch Hourn, Knoydart, Highland
Camera: Canon EOS1N;
Lens: EF 28-70 f2.8L USM
Barrisdale Bay is the starting point for Knoydart's three Munros, Ladhar Bheinn, Luinne Bheinn and Meall Bhuidhe, and can be reached by an 8km (5 mile) coastal walk from Kinloch Hourn. Although once a thriving township, Barrisdale Bay now just holds a roofless church.

pages 200–201
Loch Beinn a Mheadhoin, Fasknakyle Forest, Glen Affric, Highland
Camera: Fuji GX617; Lens: SWD90mm f5.6
With remnants of the Old Caledon Forest and native birch, Glen Affric is one of the finest glens in Scotland. The headwaters of the River Affric rise in the remote corrie of the Kintail mountains and flow down to a great confluence of streams and glens. Photographing at dawn, I waited until the mist burnt off in the morning sun.

pages 202–203
Sgurr na Ciste Duibhe, Sgurr na Carnach and Sgurr Fhuaran, Kintail, Highland
Camera: Fuji GX617; Lens: SWD90mm f5.6
Kintail is the epitome of the Scottish Highlands. For me it has an enigmatic quality partly ancient in kind, like a place lost in time. I shot this image at dawn on the ridge of the Five Sisters traverse, having waited for the cloud plume on Sgurr Fhuaran to clear the summit.

pages 204–205
Sandwood Bay and Sandwood Loch, Highland
Camera: Fuji GX617; Lens: SWD90mm f5.6
Bordered by dramatically eroded cliffs and backed by dynamic sand dunes, Sandwood Bay occupies a coastline that curves away gracefully to the most north-westerly point on mainland Britain. It is wild land, but not a wilderness, and the evidence of people who lived here before is all around – from prehistoric times to the Highland Clearances and on to the 20th century.

pages 206–207
Beinn Dearg Mor, Beinn Dearg Bheag,
Loch na Sealga, Fisherfield Forest, Highland
Camera: Hasselbald X Pan II; Lens: 30mm f5.6
Photographed from the summit of Sgurr Fiona
(3472ft/1059m) on An Teallach, the two rivers
Abhainn Strath na Sealga and Abhainn Gleann na
Muice flow to Loch na Sealga. These rivers will be
familiar to walkers who have crossed them in spate
during the winter months. The pain can linger for
days!

page 208
Snow and rocks, River Glascarnoch,
Garve, Highland
Camera: Linhof Technikardan 5x4;
Lens: Schneider Super-Angulon XL 90mm f5.6
Originating from Loch Glascarnoch, the River
Glascarnoch flows through a number of stretches
featuring huge boulders. Many of these boulders are
covered in crottle lichens (Parmelia saxatilis), once
used to dye sheep's wool. Loch Glascarnoch is on the
approach to the easterly Fannichs, a group of
mountains consisting of nine Munros.

page 209
Waterfall, River Shiel, Glen Shiel,
Kintail, Highland
Camera: Ebony 45SU;
Lens: APO Symmar 180mm f5.6
In a series of falls below Shiel Bridge, the River
Shiel cascades down steep slopes – above which
stands the starting point for the traverse of the Five
Sisters. Precipitous sides culminate at the Bealach
an Lapain; beyond, a grassy ridge rises over two
minor tops to Sgurr na Ciste Duibhe followed by
Sgurr Fhuaran, the two Munros on the ridge.

pages 210–211
Liathach and Loch Clair, Glen Torridon,
Highland
Camera: Fuji GX617; Lens: W180mm f6.7
During an unprecedented period of stable weather in
early autumn, I finally managed to capture this
scene with the foliage intact. Normally autumnal
weather windows appear after the wind and frost
have denuded the trees of their vibrant colour. I shot
more images in four days than I have ever shot
before in the Highlands.

pages 212–213
Beinn Sgritheall, Loch Hourn,
Knoydart, Highland
Camera: Linhof 617S;
Lens: Schneider Super-Angulon 90mm f5.6
Beinn Sgritheall rises directly from the north shore
of Loch Hourn to a height of 3195ft (974m). Its
northern flanks contain numerous corries, whilst the
southern flanks above the Loch include steep crags
and scree slopes. The name Beinn Sgritheall is
derived from the Gaelic for 'hill of screes'.

pages 214–215
Boulder field, Slioch, Letterewe Forest,
Loch Maree, Highland
Camera: Linhof 617S;
Lens: Schneider Super-Angulon 90mm f5.6
Like the upper parts of Slioch, this boulder field is
composed of Torridonian sandstone. Laid down when
the ice sheet retreated, the giant boulders seem like a
giant gallery dedicated to shape and form. The
underlying rock of Slioch is Lewisian Gneiss, one of
the oldest known, formed 3000 million years ago. The
sedimentary Torridonian sandstone is more recent at
around 1000 million years.

pages 216–217
Sgurr na Ciste Duibhe and Saileag from
Faochag, Kintail, Highland
Camera: Linhof 617S;
Lens: Schneider Super-Angulon 90mm f5.6
The mountains stretching along the north side of
Glen Shiel form a barrier some 10 miles (16km)
long. The peaks at the north-west end of this long
ridge are known as the Five Sisters of Kintail,
although only two are Munros. One feature of these
mountains is that they rise for over 3000ft (914m)
from the glen floor at an average angle of 30°.

page 218
Caledonian pine, Glen Affric, Highland
Camera: Hasselblad 503CX;
Lens: Zeiss Sonnar CF 150mm f4
Although much of the country was once covered by
Caledonian woodlands (a mix of Scots pine, oak,
silver birch, willow, alder and rowan, with heather
underfoot), deforestation reduced this mighty forest
to a few small pockets. The ambitious Millennium
Forest project is helping to restore native woodlands
on hundreds of sites across Scotland.

page 219
Cul Beag and Stac Pollaidh,
Inverpolly Nature Reserve, Highland
Camera: Hasselblad 503CX;
Lens: Zeiss Sonnar CF 250mm f4
Knockan Crag is situated above the main road
between Coigach and Assynt, next to Lochan an Ais,
and gives a comprehensive panorama to the west
towards Cul Mor, Stac Pollaidh and Ben Mor
Coigach. The Moine Thrust, a massive fault which
shaped much of the landscape we see today, lies
between dark rocks and white Durness limestone.

pages 220–221
Beinn Alligin, Upper Loch Torridon, Highland
Camera: Fuji GX617; Lens: SWD90mm f5.6
Carved with elegant corries, Beinn Alligin seems to
transcend the surrounding landscape with a special
dignity. Compared with the visual mass of the
Torridonian leviathans, Liathach and Beinn Eighe,
Beinn Alligin suggests a feminine character. Whilst
I have photographed her many times, the conditions
on this October evening were perfect for capturing
my favourite Scottish mountain.

pages 222–223
Suilven, Inverpolly Nature Reserve, Highland
Camera: Linhof 617S;
Lens: Schneider Super-Angulon 90mm f5.6
Suilven is the most westerly of the Assynt mountains
and dominates the surrounding landscape. It has a
remarkable appearance of changing shape when
viewed from different directions – from the west it
appears as a great rounded dome, from the east the
ridge is greatly foreshortened and from the north and
south the entire linear ridge is unfolded.

pages 224–225
River Bran, Strath Bran Forest, Highland
Camera: Linhof 617S;
Lens: Schneider Super-Angulon 90mm f5.6
Rising in Loch a' Chroisg, the River Bran flows 10
miles (16km) eastwards through Strath Bran to
enter Loch Achanalt, Loch a'Chuilinn and eventually
Loch Luichart. On the expansive moorland between
Garve and Achnasheen, hundreds of red deer are
often seen grazing during the winter months.

pages 230–231
Loch Dubh, Isle of Islay, Argyll & Bute
Camera: Linhof 617S;
Lens: Schneider Super-Angulon 90mm f5.6
The peatlands, farmlands and woodlands on Islay
support a wide variety of birds including lapwings,
redshanks and snipe, and the nights often resound to
the call of the corncrake. Hen harriers nest on the
moor, while hunting golden eagles and peregrines
can be seen all year round.

pages 232–233
Saligo Bay, Isle of Islay, Argyll & Bute
Camera: Linhof 617S;
Lens: Schneider Super-Angulon 90mm f5.6
Separated geologically from the rest of Islay by a
major break in the rocks, the Gruinart Fault passes
from Loch Indaal through the narrow neck of land
to Loch Gruinart. The rocks found on the Rhinns of
Islay and at Saligo Bay are particularly old, formed
around 2400 million years ago, making them the
oldest in Scotland bar the rocks of Lewis in the
Outer Hebrides.

pages 234–235
Ben More and Eorsa Island,
Loch na Keal, Isle of Mull, Argyll & Bute
Camera: Linhof 617S;
Lens: Schneider Super-Angulon 90mm f5.6
The view south-east across Loch na Keal and Eorsa
Island to Ben More and the Gribun Cliffs. Loch na
Keal is a large sea loch which extends far inland,
almost dissecting the island as it reaches a point
only 3 miles (5km) from the eastern coast. Rising to
3168ft (966m), Ben More is the highest peak on the
island and the most westerly Munro.

pages 236–237
Lichens and boulder, Ben More,
Isle of Mull, Argyll & Bute
Camera: Linhof 617S;
Lens: Schneider Super-Angulon 90mm f5.6
A lichen-covered boulder near the Abhainn na h-
Uamha, which rises in Gleann na Beinne Fada on
Ben More. The rock was visually striking and I
framed the image vertically to include the mountain
summit, covered in a mantle of angular screes.

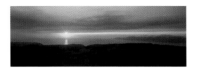 

page 238
**Paps of Jura from Foreland,
Isle of Islay, Argyll & Bute**
Camera: Hasselblad 503CX;
Lens: Zeiss Planar CF 250mm f4
Located in the southern part of the island, the Paps of Jura consist of the peaks of Beinn an Oir (Hill of Gold), Beinn a' Chaolais (Hill of the Narrows) and Beinn Shiantaidh (Holy Hill). Their rounded domes dominate the island and form one of the most prominent features on the western seaboard.

page 239
**Ben Hiant, Ardnamurchan,
Sound of Mull, Isle of Mull, Argyll & Bute**
Camera: Hasselblad 500CM;
Lens: Zeiss Distagon CF 50mm f4
By studying the distribution of Ardnamurchan's cone-sheets and ring-dykes, geologists have been able to identify a former volcanic centre around Ben Hiant. Dykes form when magma is intruded upwards into long, linear, vertical cracks in the earth's crust, typically created through crustal stretching.

pages 240–241
**Ardnamurchan Point from Mishnish,
Isle of Mull, Argyll & Bute**
Camera: Linhof 617S;
Lens: Schneider Super-Angulon 90mm f5.6
Ardnamurchan is the most westerly point of the British mainland and I set up the camera in anticipation of a big sunset. It had been an overcast day, giving little scope for photography, but there was light on the horizon – a narrow band, clouds-free, through which the sun would drop. When it eventually did so, it was like a giant theatre lamp illuminating the landscape.

pages 242–243
**Sea spray and basalt, Isle of Staffa,
Argyll & Bute**
Camera: Linhof 617S;
Lens: Schneider Super-Angulon 90mm f5.6
Staffa is unique because of its geology. The island is composed of hexagonal basalt columns set vertically, seen most clearly in Fingal's Cave, where the walls rise 40ft (12m). I wanted to shoot an image that would capture the timeless relationship between the basalt strata and the sea.

pages 244–245
**Marsco and Beinn Dearg Mhor,
Broadford Bay, Isle of Skye, Highland**
Camera: Linhof 617S;
Lens: Schneider Super-Angulon 90mm f5.6
Dominating the landscape between Broadford and Sligachan, the Red Hills consist of igneous rocks and contrast starkly with the darker, jagged peaks of the Cuillin and their outliers. Broadford Bay looks out into the Inner Sound, towards the islands of Scalpay, Longay and Pabay.

pages 246–247
**Old Man of Storr and satellites,
Isle of Skye, Highland**
Camera: Linhof 617S;
Lens: Schneider Super-Angulon 90mm f5.6
Overlooking the Sound of Raasay, The Old Man of Storr is one of the geological curiosities of the Trotternish Ridge. Composed of grey basalt, the Old Man is the largest of the monolithic pinnacles, at 160ft (50m). On this occasion the atmosphere was haunting, with the silence broken only by the sporadic croaking of two ravens nesting in the main pinnacle.

page 248
**Bla Bheinn and Gharb Bheinn,
Loch Slapin, Isle of Skye, Highland**
Camera: Arca Swiss F Metric 6x9;
Lens: Schneider Super-Angulon XL 90mm f5.6
Near the village of Torrin, superb views of Bla Bheinn and the other Cuillin outliers are possible across Loch Slapin. Geologically, Blaven consists primarily of gabbro sliced by sheets of dolerite, and in common with other mountains in the Cuillin, basalt dykes. This combination of rock has weathered at different rates giving Blaven its distinctive look.

page 249
**The Cuillin, Loch Scavaig,
Isle of Skye, Highland**
Camera: Arca Swiss F Metric 6x9;
Lens: Schneider Super-Angulon XL 58mm f5.6
Loch Scavaig is one of three main gateways to the Cuillin. The other two, Sligachan and Glen Brittle, are a little less spectacular and do not lead directly into the heart of the range like Scavaig. Here a spherical rock lies in stark contrast to the jagged Cuillin ridge

pages 250–251
Sgurr nan Gillean, Black Cuillin, Isle of Skye, Highland
Camera: Fuji GX617; Lens: W180mm f6.7
The Cuillin is arguably the finest collection of mountains in the British Isles and as such has become a Mecca for climbers. The magnificent peak of Sgurr nan Gillean commands a relatively isolated position at the end of the main ridge, accentuating its grandeur. Photographed at sunset from an outlier, the sky turned hues of yellow and crimson.

pages 252–253
Sgurr an Fheadain, Bidean Druim nan Ramh, Coire na Creiche, Isle of Skye, Highland
Camera: Linhof 617S;
Lens: Schneider Super-Angulon 90mm f5.6
The famous Waterpipe Gully, a cleft on the face of Sgurr an Fheadain at the end of this route, dominates the view of the Black Cuillin from the path as it crosses the floor of Glenbrittle. As the path begins to climb alongside the Allt Coir a' Mhadaidh, the river features a series of pools, gullies and waterfalls known as the Fairy Pools.

pages 254–255
The Quiraing, Trotternish Ridge, from the Storr, Isle of Skye, Highland
Camera: Linhof 617S;
Lens: Schneider Super-Angulon 90mm f5.6
The scenery of the east-facing Trotternish escarpment is spectacular and features landmarks including The Storr and The Quiraing. The three principal elements of The Quirang are The Needle, The Prison and The Table, which consist of Jurassic sedimentary sequences overlain by thick Tertiary lava flows.

pages 256–257
Beinn Sgritheall and Ladhar Bheinn, Loch Hourn, Sound of Sleat, Isle of Skye, Highland
Camera: Fuji GX617; Lens: W180mm f6.7
The view south-east from Loch na Dal across the Sound of Sleat to Loch Hourn. To the east the sun rises on the precipitous slopes of Beinn Sgritheall, while standing opposite, Ladhar Bheinn's summit ridge is in cloud. Ladhar Bheinn is Scotland's most westerly mainland Munro, situated in the Knoydart peninsula.

page 258
Traigh Nisabost, Sound of Taransay, Isle of Harris, Western Isles
Camera: Hasselblad 500CM;
Lens: Zeiss Distagon CF 50mm f4
South of Luskentyre, Traigh Nisabost is an area of shell beach where rock intrusions create natural edges in the landscape. Combined with the edges of light and shadow, these features present the possibility of powerful visual statements. The edges of the world are the most interesting – places where land meets sea or mountains meet sky.

page 259
Bla Bheinn and Clach Glas, Cuillin, Isle of Skye, Highland
Camera: Hasselblad 503CX;
Lens: Zeiss Planar CF 150mm f4
Blaven is the most southerly Red Cuillin, separated from the main Cuillin range by Glen Sligachan, and the highest of the group of surrounding mountains. Photographed here at dusk, the summit ridge to Clach Glas, nicknamed The Matterhorn of Skye, can be combined with the ascent of the main summit with a little moderate climbing.

pages 260–261
The Cuillin, Loch Scavaig, Isle of Skye, Highland
Camera: Linhof 617S;
Lens: Schneider Super-Angulon 90mm f5.6
Scotland's most renowned and spectacular mountain range, the Cuillin of Skye, could soon be gifted to the Scottish people by their owner, John MacLeod of MacLeod. Parts of the Cuillin already belong to the John Muir Trust, a conservation charity, and to gift the central part of the mountain range to the nation would open up the prospect of managing the entire Cuillin range in the public interest.

pages 262–263
The Storr, Trotternish Ridge, Isle of Skye, Highland
Camera: Fuji GX617; Lens: EBC Fujinon T300 f8
Notwithstanding the Cuillin, the most impressive hills in Skye are in Trotternish where the longest continuous ridge on the island has its highest point on The Storr. Below, formed by a series of landslides that exposed the basalt lavas, the Old Man of Storr's dramatic pinnacle makes a distinctive landmark.

pages 264–265
Sron Scourst and Uisgnaval Mor,
Forest of Harris, Isle of Harris, Western Isles
Camera: Linhof 617S;
Lens: Schneider Super-Angulon 90mm f5.6
The Harris Hills were formed on the oldest rock in
the world, Lewisian Gneiss, and present a strange
and awe-inspiring lunar landscape. I continue to
have great difficulty grasping the concept of rocks
that were formed 3000 million years ago.

pages 266–267
Traigh Nisabost, Sound of Taransay,
Isle of Harris, Western Isles
Camera: Linhof 617S;
Lens: Schneider Super-Angulon 90mm f5.6
This image is a personal favourite and was shot
through frustration. The morning had dawned bright
and clear, but an Atlantic front approached with
mist and cloud bases dropping below the summits. I
arrived late at this location and hurried to catch the
last rays of sunlight illuminating the beach, but
failed and pressed the shutter in frustration.
Ironically the muted colours create the harmony.

page 268
Bioda Bhuidhe and the Totternish Ridge,
The Quiraing, Isle of Skye, Highland
Camera: Ebony 45SU;
Lens: Schneider APO Symmar 180mm f5.6
The sea eagle has begun to nest again in Trotternish
after an absence of 100 years. It is a result of their
recent deliberate re-introduction to the Isle of Rum,
from where they have found their way to Skye.
Another recently re-introduced bird of prey which
can be seen in Skye is the red kite.

page 269
Waterfall, Allt Coire nam Bruadaran, Marsco,
Isle of Skye, Highland
Camera: Ebony 45SU;
Lens: Schneider APO Symmar 180mm f5.6
If you walk south from the Sligachan Hotel, the
Cuillin main ridge is to your right. To your left is a
succession of fine and varied hills – Glamaig,
Marsco, Garbh Bheinn, Sgurr nan Each and finally
Bla Bheinn, one of Scotland's most celebrated and
beautiful mountains. This land is owned by the John
Muir Trust, about 46 square miles (12,000ha) in
all, with many miles of coast, and it continues down
the Strathaird peninsula to Elgol.

pages 270–271
Cleiseval and Uisgnaval Mor, Traigh Rosamol,
Isle of Harris, Western Isles
Camera: Linhof 617S;
Lens: Schneider Super-Angulon 90mm f5.6
The North Harris landscape is spectacularly
beautiful. It is the most mountainous region in the
Western Isles and includes the Sron Ulladail
overhang and the highest hill, Clisham
(2622ft/799m). Its rugged upland and oceanic
habitats provide a haven for wildlife, and the wild
core is completely uninhabited.

pages 272–273
**Traigh Luskentyre and Corran Seilebost,
Isle of Harris, Western Isles**
Camera: Linhof 617S;
Lens: Schneider Super-Angulon 90mm f5.6
There is nothing like seeing the lime-rich soils of the
coast in full bloom with carpet machair flowers. With
up to 45 species in any square metre, it presents an
astonishing riot of colour. Here are some examples of
what you can expect to see: orchids, yellow iris,
pansies, poppies, sea bindweed, Irish ladies tressels,
yellow rattle, red clover, daisies, marram.

pages 274–275
**Isle of Taransay, Traigh Seilebost,
Isle of Harris, Western Isles**
Camera: Linhof 617S;
Lens: Schneider Super-Angulon 90mm f5.6
Illuminated from below by shell sand, the sea takes
on shades of turquoise that contrast with the blonde
beaches and blue skies. Set alongside machair dunes
and the mountainous backdrop of North Harris, the
landscape is incredibly diverse.

pages 276–277
**Loch na Cleavag, Cravadale, Isle of Harris,
Western Isles**
Camera: Linhof 617S;
Lens: Schneider Super-Angulon 90mm f5.6
One of the remotest locations in Harris, Loch na
Cleavag is accessed by an old stalkers' track which
follows the hillside east from Hushinish. Beyond the
stretch of water lies the deserted island of Scarp and
further east, out on the horizon, St Kilda's stacs are
just visible. During the day I watched an otter
feeding on a sea urchin and a golden eagle soaring
in Glen Cravadale.

page 278
**Boulder and lichens, Elgol, Isle of Skye,
Highland**
Camera: Ebony 45SU;
Lens: Schneider Super-Angulon XL 90mm f5.6
Encrusted with lichens like an artist's palette, a
boulder reflects the shades of the surrounding
landscape. A number of environmental factors
including humidity, temperature and rock pH are
essential to the success of lichens, which are
abundant in the inter-tidal zone.

page 279
**Loch Airigh na h'Achlais, Loch Druidibeag Nature
Reserve, South Uist, Western Isles**
Camera: Ebony 45SU;
Lens: Schneider Super-Angulon XL 72mm f5.6
The area around Loch Druidibeag is a National Nature
Reserve with many different habitats, including freshwater,
brackish lagoon, dune, machair, peatland and scrub
woodland. The loch itself is shallow but very large, and has
numerous islands: one of these is home to a resident colony
of herons. The greylag geese which breed around the loch
contribute to the resident population that remain in the
Uists all year.

ACKNOWLEDGEMENTS

I would like to thank Geraldine, my wife, for her patience and understanding during the years I worked on this book. Also to my daughter Alexandra and my son Laurence who selflessly accepted that I couldn't always be there. In Scotland, climatic conditions change quickly and the need to react to a stable weather period is essential. Trips planned at short notice with an imminent departure left many family and social engagements in turmoil.

Those individuals involved in the great outdoors acknowledge the importance of equipment and advice and I would like to thank the management of Tiso's for their support and encouragement during this project.

The images themselves would not exist without the technology on which I depend and I would like to acknowledge Fuji Photo Film (UK) Ltd for their cameras and film, Hasselblad (UK) Ltd, Canon UK Ltd and Robert White Photographic.

Finally to Pete Duncan and Nova Jayne Heath of Constable & Robinson whose enthusiasm and vision for the project was a constant source of encouragement.

Further information about the work of Colin Prior can be found at www.colinprior.com Biographical information, subscription to an on-line newsletter with regular updates of new projects, and the opportunity to visit the store where the full range of prints, calendars and books can be found.

Hugh Prior

Much of my time in the mountains has been spent with my father. We have shared many of the high points of mountain experience in remote locations at dusk and dawn. Whether under canvas, in a bothy or in some grim motel on the edge of nowhere, we have developed a special relationship. What to others may have seemed ludicrous was always accepted, without protest, by my father, whose spiritual and physical support has been a constant source of encouragement. In Scotland, Pakistan, Nepal, India and Patagonia his unerring energy has helped me to capture the dramatic mountain landscapes of the world and I am indebted to him.